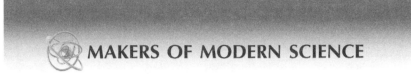

MAKERS OF MODERN SCIENCE

Rita
Levi-Montalcini

MAKERS OF MODERN SCIENCE

Rita Levi-Montalcini

Discoverer of Nerve Growth Factor

LISA YOUNT

CHELSEA HOUSE
P U B L I S H E R S
An imprint of Infobase Publishing

RITA LEVI-MONTALCINI: Discoverer of Nerve Growth Factor

Chelsea House
An imprint of Infobase Publishing
132 West 31st Street
New York NY 10001

Library of Congress Cataloging-in-Publication Data

Yount, Lisa.
    Rita Levi-Montalcini : discoverer of nerve growth factor / Lisa Yount.
      p. cm.—(Makers of modern science)
    Includes bibliographical references and index.
    ISBN 13: 978-0-8160-6171-6
    ISBN 10: 0-8160-6171-8
    1. Levi-Montalcini, Rita. 2. Women scientists—Italy—Biography—Juvenile literature. 3. Neurologists—Italy—Biography—Juvenile literature. I. Title. II. Series.
Q143.L47.Y58 2009
573.8092—dc22 [B]   2008015472

Chelsea House books are available at special discounts when purchased in bulk quantities for businesses, associations, institutions, or sales promotions. Please call our Special Sales Department in New York at (212) 967-8800 or (800) 322-8755.

You can find Chelsea House on the World Wide Web at
http://www.chelseahouse.com

Text design by Kerry Casey
Cover design by Salvatore Luongo
Illustrations by Melissa Ericksen
Photo research by Suzanne M. Tibor

Printed in the United States of America

Bang KT 10 9 8 7 6 5 4 3 2 1

This book is printed on acid-free paper and contains 30 percent postconsumer recycled content.

To Debbie,
who helped me survive a tough time

CONTENTS

PREFACE

....

Science is, above all, a great human adventure. It is the process of exploring what Albert Einstein called the "magnificent structure" of nature using observation, experience, and logic. Science comprises the best methods known to humankind for finding reliable answers about the unknown. With these tools, scientists probe the great mysteries of the universe—from black holes and star nurseries to deep-sea hydrothermal vents (and extremophile organisms that survive high temperatures to live in them); from faraway galaxies to subatomic particles such as quarks and antiquarks; from signs of life on other worlds to microorganisms such as bacteria and viruses here on Earth; from how a vaccine works to protect a child from disease to the DNA, genes, and enzymes that control traits and processes from the color of a boy's hair to how he metabolizes sugar.

Some people think that science is rigid and static, a dusty, musty set of facts and statistics to memorize for a test and then forget. Some think of science as antihuman—devoid of poetry, art, and a sense of mystery. However, science is based on a sense of wonder and is all about exploring the mysteries of life and our planet and the vastness of the universe. Science offers methods for testing and reasoning that help keep us honest with ourselves. As physicist Richard Feynman once said, science is above all a way to keep from fooling yourself—or letting nature (or others) fool you. Nothing could be more growth-oriented or more human. Science evolves continually. New bits of knowledge and fresh discoveries endlessly shed light and open perspectives. As a result, science is constantly undergoing revolutions—ever refocusing what scientists have explored before into fresh, new understanding. Scientists like to say science is self-correcting. That is, science is fallible, and scientists can be wrong. It is easy to fool yourself, and it is easy to be fooled by others, but because new facts are constantly flowing in, scientists are continually refining their work to account for as many facts as possible. So science can make mistakes, but it also can correct itself.

Sometimes, as medical scientist Jonas Salk liked to point out, good science thrives when scientists ask the right question about what they observe. "What people think of as the moment of discovery is really the discovery of the question," he once remarked.

There is no one, step-by-step "scientific method" that all scientists use. However, science requires the use of methods that are systematic, logical, and *empirical* (based on objective observation and experience). The goal of science is to explore and understand how nature works—what causes the patterns, the shapes, the colors, the textures, the consistency, the mass, and all the other characteristics of the natural universe that we see.

What is it like to be a scientist? Many people think of stereotypes of the scientist trapped in cold logic or the cartoonlike "mad" scientists. In general, these portrayals are more imagination than truth. Scientists use their brains. They are exceptionally good at logic and critical thinking. This is where the generalizations stop. Although science follows strict rules, it is often guided by the many styles and personalities of the scientists themselves, who have distinct individuality, personality, and style. What better way to explore what science is all about than through the experiences of great scientists?

Each volume of the Makers of Modern Science series presents the life and work of a prominent scientist whose outstanding contributions have garnered the respect and recognition of the world. These men and women were all great scientists, but they differed in many ways. Their approaches to the use of science were different: Niels Bohr was an atomic theorist whose strengths lay in patterns, ideas, and conceptualization, while Wernher von Braun was a hands-on scientist/engineer who led the team that built the giant rocket used by Apollo astronauts to reach the Moon. Some's genius was sparked by solitary contemplation—geneticist Barbara McClintock worked alone in fields of maize and sometimes spoke to no one all day long. Others worked as members of large, coordinated teams. Oceanographer Robert Ballard organized oceangoing ship crews on submersible expeditions to the ocean floor; biologist Jonas Salk established the Salk Institute to help scientists in different fields collaborate more freely and study the human body through the interrelationships of their differing knowledge and approaches. Their personal styles also differed: biologist Rita Levi-Montalcini enjoyed wearing chic dresses and makeup; McClintock was sunburned and wore baggy denim jeans and an oversized shirt; nuclear physicist Richard Feynman was a practical joker and an energetic bongo drummer.

The scientists chosen represent a spectrum of disciplines and a diversity of approaches to science as well as lifestyles. Each biography explores the scientist's younger years along with education and growth as a scientist; the experiences, research, and contributions of the maturing scientist; and the course of the path to recognition. Each volume also explores the nature of science and its unique usefulness for studying the universe and contains sidebars covering related facts or profiles of interest, introductory coverage of the scientist's field, line illustrations and photographs, a time line, a glossary of related scientific terms, and a list of further resources including books, Web sites, periodicals, and associations.

The volumes in the Makers of Modern Science series offer a factual look at the lives and exciting contributions of the profiled scientists in the hope that readers will see science as a uniquely human quest to understand the universe and that some readers may be inspired to follow in the footsteps of these great scientists.

ACKNOWLEDGMENTS

I would like to thank Frank K. Darmstadt for his help and suggestions, Suzie Tibor for her hard work in rounding up the photographs, and, as always, my husband, Harry Henderson, for being the "factor" that provides so much of what I need for my survival and growth.

INTRODUCTION

"**I** have never become a scientist. I am more of an artist," Rita Levi-Montalcini said in an interview quoted in *Candid Science II: Conversations with Famous Biomedical Scientists.* This might seem a strange statement from a woman who won the Nobel Prize in physiology or medicine—but perhaps it was not so strange for Levi-Montalcini, because she came from a family of artists. Her twin sister, Paola, was a famous painter and sculptor; her brother, Gino, was an equally well-known architect. Her mother had painted as well.

It is clear from Levi-Montalcini's own writing and from comments that others have made about her that her perception was correct: She did approach science from an artist's point of view. In her autobiography, *In Praise of Imperfection,* she described nerve growth factor (NGF), the substance whose discovery brought her the coveted prize, not as a mere biological substance but as a mysterious masked figure—first revealed to her in the wild atmosphere of carnival in Rio de Janeiro—whom she had spent her life pursuing. She spoke often of making intuitive leaps that showed her in an hour a picture of the nervous system's behavior that would take her years of painstaking experiments to prove scientifically. "Something . . . comes to my mind, and I know it's true," she said in another interview quoted in Sharon McGrayne's *Nobel Prize Women in Science.* "It is a particular gift, in the subconscious." According to Carol Kahn, writing in *Omni* magazine in 1988, Stanley Cohen, NGF's codiscoverer and fellow recipient of the Nobel award, greatly admired Levi-Montalcini's intuition, which he saw as the perfect complement to his own step-by-step approach.

The artist in Levi-Montalcini was attracted by the art in nature. "The beauty of the nervous system" was what drew her to its study, she said, beginning in medical school when she first glimpsed the system's complex spiderweb of interlocking cells and fibers under the microscope. NGF proved to be one of the architects of that system, guiding its cells to their final goals as organisms develop before birth and shaping its responses to outside forces in adults.

Both artists and scientists do their best work in a timeless place, mentally far away from the everyday events going on around them. At the start of her career, Levi-Montalcini protected herself by retreating to that quiet space during a time that was anything but quiet: World War II, when Italy, her homeland, was ruled by a dictatorial government that threatened the livelihood and even the lives of those who shared her Jewish ancestry. Forced out of her job by the government's anti-Semitic laws, she built a simple home laboratory "not unlike a convent cell" and in it began the experiments that would lead her down the long path to scientific fame. Throughout her life, she overcame obstacles, she said, by "underestimating" them—or rather, perhaps, by seeing beyond them, as an artist does.

A great work of art opens up vistas that stretch far beyond what its creator originally conceived. Other artists, bringing their own intuition to it, can build upon it to produce new works that move in different directions. This also happens with great discoveries in science. Levi-Montalcini found NGF by seeking to learn how the nervous system developed, but her discovery ultimately led to much more than that. Building upon it, she, Cohen, and a host of other researchers unearthed a whole class of compounds that are intimately involved in every stage of a cell's or an organism's life, from conception to death. The biochemical world revealed by Rita Levi-Montalcini's artistic creativity is just beginning to be explored.

As this volume in Makers of Modern Science shows, Rita Levi-Montalcini needed more than an artist's inspiration to achieve the success that eventually brought her a Nobel Prize. She also needed incredible persistence and faith in herself. These qualities, which she said in her autobiography that she inherited from her father, helped her to break free of the expectations that that same father (and early-20th-century Italian society in general) had for her as a woman and to obtain a medical degree instead of a wedding ring. They allowed her to continue her research in defiance of the persecution of Jews

xvi   RITA LEVI-MONTALCINI

in Fascist Italy in the late 1930s and early 1940s, which cost her her job and threatened her life.

During the 30 years Levi-Montalcini spent at Washington University in St. Louis, persistence and the conviction that she was on the right track kept her pursuing the mysterious substance she had discovered, which made nerves sprout from tissue in an explosive halo of growth, even when others questioned her findings. The same qualities supported her in her later life, when she returned to Italy to found a new laboratory and eventually move beyond research into new fields, including politics and philanthropy. As an artist and a science writer, I have been inspired by Levi-Montalcini's combination of intuition, scientific logic, confidence, and persistence in the face of obstacles, and I hope that young people, whatever their career choices, will find her life story inspiring as well.

Shaping a Life

As an adult, Rita Levi-Montalcini discovered a substance that, like a skilled native guide shepherding a party of travelers, steers the cells of unborn animals' developing nervous systems to their goals in different parts of the animals' bodies. In her childhood, her own mind and personality were shaped and guided by equally powerful forces in her environment, beginning with her father and her society's expectations of the role that women should play. Unlike the nerve cells she later studied, however, Levi-Montalcini refused to follow the path that her world had laid out for her. Instead, she took on the task of guiding her own development.

A Colorful Family

Rita Levi-Montalcini was born on April 22, 1909, in Turin, a prosperous industrial city in northern Italy, not far from the border

Turin is the capital of the Piedmont region of northern Italy. This photo, taken from the Mount of the Capuchins, shows Turin as it looked around the time Rita Levi-Montalcini was born. (Library of Congress)

with Switzerland. Capital of the Piedmont ("foot of the mountains") region, Turin lies along the Po, Italy's largest river. When Italy was first united, in 1861, Turin was its capital for four years. At the time of Rita's birth, the city boasted about 430,000 people.

Levi-Montalcini's father, Adamo Levi, was an electrical engineer and factory owner. (Rita changed her name to Levi-Montalcini as an adult to honor her mother's family as well as her father's.) His first factory, in Bari on southern Italy's warm Adriatic coast, made and sold ice, an essential tool for preserving food in the days before refrigeration. Until this factory was built, local businessmen brought snow down from the nearby mountains each winter and stored it underground before selling it to the town's butchers. In her autobiography, *In Praise of Imperfection,* Levi-Montalcini wrote that her father's ice factory upset these rivals so much at first that they threatened Levi with death if he did not leave the city. The ice factory prospered, however, and in time Levi built a second factory, also in Bari, that distilled alcohol from carobs, the seeds or pods of tropical trees. During Rita's childhood, the Levi family lived a comfortable life.

As his daughter saw him, Adamo Levi was a formidable man. His bristling moustache scratched Rita's face, which she used as an excuse not to kiss him. (In fact, she preferred not to touch or kiss anyone. She even sometimes blew kisses to her mother, whom she liked much better than her father, rather than kissing her directly.) His sudden rages, which had earned him the nickname of "Damino (a nickname for Adamo) the Terrible" among his brothers and sisters, terrified her. At the same time, she admired him greatly. She later said that she had gotten "tenacity, energy, and ingenuity . . . [and] seriousness and dedication to work" from him.

Adamo's powerful personality guaranteed that he would occupy the position in his family that the society of the time expected of him: unquestioned head of the household. Even though he was often away from home, supervising his two factories, he determined everything about the way his four children were raised, down to the design of his youngest daughters' hats. His wife, the gentle Adele Montalcini, nine years younger, seldom argued with him—a state of affairs that Rita disliked. "Ever since my childhood, I had strongly resented the different roles played by my father and mother in all family decisions," Sharon McGrayne's *Nobel Prize Women in Science* quotes Levi-Montalcini as saying. "I adored my mother and rebelled against this difference, which I also feared for myself as a future housewife." In spite of this unequal relationship, Rita wrote in the brief autobiography published in *Les Prix Nobel, The Nobel Prizes 1986* that she was surrounded in childhood by "a wonderful family atmosphere, filled with love and reciprocal devotion."

After her father, the family member who probably had the greatest effect on Rita's development was her twin sister, Paola. Throughout their lives, the two sisters had the special bond that twins often share; in a 1988 interview for *Omni* magazine, Levi-Montalcini called Paola "a part of myself." Nonetheless, as she also pointed out in her autobiography, she and Paola were fraternal rather than identical twins, born from two eggs that had developed at the same time in their mother's womb. They looked quite different, with Paola echoing her father's dark coloring and Rita, by contrast, taking after her blond mother and maternal grandmother. Their interests were different, too: From her early youth, Paola showed great talent as an artist—an ability she may have inherited from her mother, who also painted—whereas Rita had no idea where her abilities lay.

Rita also admired her older brother, Gino, and older sister, Anna, but she saw less of them than of Paola. As a compromise between his own desire to become a sculptor and his father's hope that he would study engineering, Gino became an architect, eventually one of the best known in Italy. (Ruby Rohrlich, writing in the Winter 2000 issue of the quarterly journal *Judaism,* called him "one of the most prominent Italian architects of the postwar period.") Levi-Montalcini wrote in *Women Scientists: The Road to Liberation,* however, that Gino never stopped wishing he could have been a sculptor. Anna, whom the family called Nina, dreamed of becoming a writer like the Nobel Prize–winning (in 1909) Swedish author Selma Lagerlöf, but in the end she adopted the more conventional role of wife and mother.

Rita Levi-Montalcini was a timid child, afraid of adults, mechanical objects, and even "monsters that might suddenly pop out of the dark and throw themselves upon me," she wrote. If she had to go down the long hallway between the children's playroom and her bedroom after dark, she asked Paola to come with her for protection. Her father called her his "shrinking violet." Yet her mother saw a different side of her, maintaining, "Rita is not easily frightened." She

As a child, Rita Levi-Montalcini was outwardly timid but, she said later, "very strong inside." She was about 11 years old when this photograph was taken. (SPL/Photo Researchers, Inc.)

pointed out that Rita played with animals, even large ones, without fear. The fact that animals were living creatures made the difference, Levi-Montalcini guessed later. She told *Vogue* writer Frederika Randall in 1987 that, in spite of her surface timidity, she had been "very strong inside" as a child.

The Levis' Jewish heritage played a much less important part in shaping Rita than the personalities in her family. She went to celebrations of Passover and a few other religious holidays at the homes of her mother's relatives, but her own parents did not attend a synagogue or follow most Jewish traditions. Like most Italian Jews of their time, the Levis had Catholic friends, as well as Jewish ones, and were well integrated into Italian society. Adamo Levi did not deny his family's roots, but he always told his children to say, if asked about their religion, that they were freethinkers. He said that Rita and her brother and sisters could choose any religion they wished— or none—when they grew up.

The fact that the Levi family was Jewish did not bother most of their friends and acquaintances, whether these were Jewish or not. After all, there had been Levis in Turin since the days of the Roman Empire. Levi-Montalcini wrote with irritation about one governess who had told the children frightening stories about Jews and tried to convert them to Catholicism, but this woman apparently was unusual. According to Levi-Montalcini, during her own childhood and her parents' youth, Italy was generally tolerant of Jews. Italy had had two part-Jewish prime ministers in a row (Sidney Sonnino and Luigi Luzzatti) between 1909 and 1911, and the citizens of Rome had elected a Jewish mayor, Ernesto Nathan, in 1907. This liberal attitude contrasted sharply with the severe anti-Semitism in other parts of Europe, such as Russia, where Jews were isolated in ghetto settlements and sometimes massacred.

Politics and world events played little part in shaping Rita Levi-Montalcini's childhood. A minor exception was World War I, which Italy entered on the side of the Allies (France and England) in 1915, when Rita was in first grade. During the war, she adopted the patriotic attitude taught to all the children in her class. She was especially impressed by visits from her schoolmistress's sister, a Red Cross nurse, and "hoped the war would last long enough that I, too, could join the Red Cross nurses and take part in some heroic action on the battlefield." She rejoiced with her classmates when the war ended in victory for the Allied side two years later.

Preparing a New Path

Society's expectations took a turn at shaping Rita's life when she entered high school. Boys could attend either a high school that prepared them for university studies or one that set them on the road to careers in the arts and trades. The girls' high school, by contrast, trained them only for life as wives and mothers. Education in science and mathematics was totally lacking, since people expected that women would have no reason to learn these subjects. Expressing a typical Victorian view of women's place, for instance, famed British author John Ruskin had written in 1865 that a woman "ought to know [any] language, or science, only so far as may enable her to sympathize in her husband's pleasures, and in those of his best friends."

A few women did escape this pattern and obtain higher education. Two of Adamo Levi's sisters, in fact, had gone to the University of Turin: One had earned a doctorate in literature and another a doctorate in mathematics. Indeed, Levi himself held one of these sisters to be the most intelligent person in his large family. Nonetheless, he thought that their extra education had done nothing except make them unhappy, since they had been unable to pursue careers in their fields and had had trouble adjusting to their later, unavoidable domestic roles. He therefore insisted on sending all his daughters to the girls' high school. According to Rita, neither Nina nor Paola objected much to this decision, since they did not feel that a university education was necessary for writing or art. (In fact, Paola joined the studio of a well-known artist, Felice Casorati, as soon as she finished high school.) Only Rita herself wished strongly that she had had another choice.

Rita had a strong resistance to following the expected women's path. Her nervousness around other people made it hard for her to approach even other girls, let alone boys. She despised the idea of subjecting herself to a man, as a woman was expected to do in marriage. She felt no attraction to babies or desire to become a mother. She had no idea what she wanted to do instead, however.

Rita never thought about a career in science. In addition to having no chance to take science courses in the girls' high school, she was exposed constantly to the idea that women had no ability to be creators or discoverers in science or any other field. She wrote later that her boy cousins teased her by pointing out that all the most famous scientists and artists had been men. The notion that women had simply lacked the opportunity to make equal achievements did not, at the time, occur either to them or to her.

Even at age 20, as Levi-Montalcini put it in her autobiography, she still "drifted along in the dark" regarding what she wanted to do with her life. The event that shone a light into her darkness was a tragic one. Giovanna Bruttata, a woman who had lived with the Levi family and helped to raise Rita and her brother and sisters, in essence becoming a second mother to them, developed inoperable stomach cancer and died early in 1930. The loss of this beloved family friend inspired Rita, who had always had a strong desire to help others (in 2000 she told *Candid Science* author Magdolna Hargittai that one of the reasons she had not wanted to marry as a young woman was because marriage and children would have interfered with "my goal of serving people"), to decide that she wanted to become a medical doctor.

Rita knew that the first step in carrying out her plan, as in anything else, would have to be gaining her father's permission. To ease what she expected to be a difficult task, she told her mother first, and Adele, in turn, spoke to Adamo before Rita did. When Rita had her own conversation with her father, he repeated his conviction that higher education was unsuitable for a woman and would merely make her miserable. However, perhaps to his daughter's surprise, he went on to say that if she was sure that was what she wanted, he would not try to keep her from going to the university.

Rita knew that she could not enter Turin University with the limited academic preparation she had had. She would need tutoring in Greek, Latin, mathematics, basic science, and other subjects. She asked a cousin, Eugenia Lustig, to join her, and the fatherless Eugenia, facing an uncertain future of her own, was happy to do so. Two local professors provided tutoring in languages, math, and science, while the young women tackled philosophy, literature, and history on their own.

After preparing for eight months, Rita and Eugenia took entrance examinations with other "external" students—those who had studied at home rather than in regular classes. Both passed the exams easily. Indeed, despite her nervousness at being unable to answer a question about the currents in the Pacific gulf, Rita earned a higher score than anyone else who took the tests that year.

A Powerful Mentor

Rita began studying in the medical school of the venerable University of Turin, founded in 1404, in the fall of 1930. She persuaded Eugenia to do the same, although Eugenia's first interest had been mathematics. They were two of only seven women in a class of about 300. Like the other beginning students, they attended lectures in the morning and did laboratory work in the afternoon.

The course that impressed Rita the most was anatomy, the study of the body's structure. She watched dissections of corpses in the medical school's anatomy amphitheater, which had steep tiers of benches arranged in semicircles around a central spot where the dissections took place—a design that went back to the Renaissance. In the afternoon laboratory sessions, she and the other students had the chance to dissect human bodies for themselves.

Giuseppe Levi, the professor who taught the course and headed the medical school's Institute of Anatomy, was not related to Rita, yet he reminded her of her father. He, too, was a huge bear of a man, with powerful muscles honed by his hobby of mountain climbing. Like Adamo Levi, Giuseppe Levi had a terrible temper, flying into sudden rages at students whom he deemed "a pain in the neck." (One of his milder remarks was "I beg your pardon, but you are a perfect imbecile.") He was not a good lecturer, at least not in that class. His real love was the anatomy that could be seen under the microscope, not the kind that showed on the dissecting table. Nonetheless, his tremendous energy and passion for his work appealed to Rita.

During their second year in medical school, Rita and Eugenia became Levi's interns, carrying out advanced studies under his supervision. His specialty was histology, or microscopic anatomy. In order to see the structure of different body tissues under the microscope,

The Human Nervous System

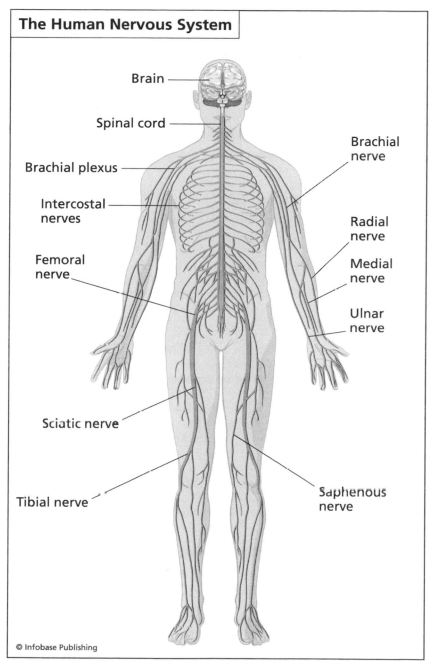

Brain

Spinal cord

Brachial nerve

Brachial plexus

Intercostal nerves

Radial nerve

Femoral nerve

Medial nerve

Ulnar nerve

Sciatic nerve

Tibial nerve

Saphenous nerve

© Infobase Publishing

Rita Levi-Montalcini studied anatomy, or the structure of the body, in medical school. Of all the body systems, the nervous system, shown here, interested her the most. The brain and spinal cord make up the central nervous system. The nerves that extend from the cord to other parts of the body are the peripheral nervous system.

Levi's students had to slice the tissues thinly and treat them with stains that brought out features within the cells. Preparing the microscope slides properly was difficult—"more of an art than a science," Levi-Montalcini wrote—and she felt that, for the most part, she had neither the skill nor the motivation to do it well (she wrote in *Neurosciences:*

Giuseppe Levi (1872–1965): Pioneer Histologist and Mentor to Nobel Prize Winners

Giuseppe Levi was one of the best-known professors of histology, or microscopic anatomy, of his time. Born in the northern Italian city of Trieste in 1872 to a family of Jewish bankers, he studied at universities in Florence and Vienna, Austria, graduating in 1895. He devoted his career to studying nerve tissue under the microscope. He adapted two new forms of technology to this science: tissue culture, or the growing of cells in laboratory dishes or tubes, and cinematography, which he used to produce time-lapse movies of nerve cell growth. He was one of the first to study mitochondria, organelles within cells that provide the cells' energy.

Levi taught at the universities of Sassari (Sardinia), Palermo (Sicily), and Turin. He became head of the Turin medical school's Institute of Normal Anatomy in 1919 and kept this post until forced out of it by anti-Jewish laws that Italy's Fascist government passed in 1938. After World War II he returned to research and teaching, focusing on the process of aging. He died of stomach cancer in January 1965.

Levi and his wife, Lidia, had five children. One of their daughters became a famous writer under her married name, Natalia Ginzburg. Some of her books, such as *Lessico Famigliare (Family Sayings)*, published in 1963, described her childhood and provided a vivid picture of the tempestuous Levi. According to Sharon McGrayne's *Nobel Prize Women in Science*, Levi-Montalcini said that Ginzburg's books reminded her of her own youth.

Giuseppe Levi's enthusiasm for science was as impressive as his rages. One of the three Nobel Prize winners he trained, Renato Dulbecco, wrote, "I think that Levi's attitude explains why the three of us ended up . . . earning the Nobel Prize. He had taught us the right attitude for doing research."

Paths of Discovery that she had "hated histology"). The one exception proved to involve a silver-containing stain used on neurons, the spiderweb-like cells of the nervous system. Rita became an expert at applying this stain, impressing even the fearsome Levi.

Around the other medical school students, Rita remained as shy as ever. She dressed very plainly, "like a nun" as *Nobel Prize Women in Science* quotes her as saying, and rejected any young men who might hint that they wanted to date her. "I wanted to spend all my time on research. I was not receptive to courtship. . . . I didn't want any contact as a woman," she recalled. Indeed, a fellow student told her later that she had seemed like "a kind of squid ready to squirt ink at anybody who came near you."

Nonetheless, Rita did make a few friends. They included fellow Levi interns Salvador Luria and Renato Dulbecco, both of whom would go on, like Levi-Montalcini herself, to win Nobel Prizes. (Dulbecco, five years younger than Levi-Montalcini, was merely an acquaintance at this time but became a close friend later.) These three and two other students, Rodolfo Amprino (Levi's favorite student, according to Levi-Montalcini) and a young man named Fazio, often met in the laboratory or in the Institute of Anatomy's library to compare notes on their projects or trade "recipes" for preparing and staining microscope slides. When doing so they tried to keep out of the path of Levi, who was likely to fly into one of his famous rages if he saw students gossiping in the library or setting their coats or other belongings on one of its tables.

Rita's second year in medical school was marred by tragedy. In May 1932 her father suffered a slight stroke, in which blood flow in his brain became temporarily blocked. He recovered, but then he began suffering the chest pains of angina, a type of heart disease. By this time, economic problems, including repeated strikes, had forced him to close his factories in Bari, and he was trying to rebuild them on a smaller scale in the outskirts of Turin. Trips to the factory site by public transit were long and tiring, but he continued to make them often (almost always accompanied by a worried Adele), refusing to let illness slow him down. Finally, at the beginning of August, he suffered a series of heart attacks that killed him. Although Rita and her father had not gotten along well while he was alive, she joined the rest of her family in mourning his loss.

Nerve Cells under Glass

Back in class, Rita had to deal with the first of several research projects that Giuseppe Levi assigned to her as an intern. Levi told Rita and Eugenia to try to find out whether the number of neurons in the sensory ganglia, small clumps of nerve cells on either side of each bone of the spinal column, was the same or different in mice from different broods. (Sensory nerves detect changes in the environment and send that information to an animal's brain.) This task involved many hours of bending over the microscope, counting thousands of cells. The work was not only boring but, Rita thought, probably use-

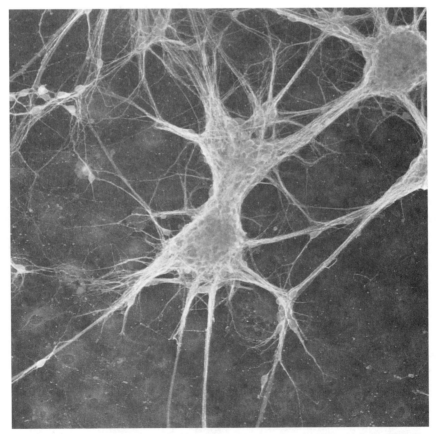

As Giuseppe Levi's intern, Rita Levi-Montalcini did several projects in which she looked at neurons, or nerve cells, under a microscope. She thought the weblike cells were beautiful. (François Paquet-Durand/Photo Researchers, Inc.)

less. She doubted that the counts could be accurate, no matter how carefully they were done. A visiting professor echoed her feelings when he said that determining the number of leaves on the trees outside the laboratory window would be just as valuable.

Levi-Montalcini concluded later that Levi's assignment raised an important question—whether the number of cells in particular parts of the nervous system was determined strictly by heredity or, instead, could be altered by factors in the environment. She felt, however, that the era's primitive preparation techniques made the question impossible to answer. She and Eugenia resisted the urge to make up whatever figures they thought would please their demanding professor, as they knew that some of the other students did, but she thought they did not gain much by their honesty.

Levi's next assignment—trying to determine how the convolutions, or folds, of the human brain were formed before birth—was not much better. The first problem with the task, Rita realized, would be finding human fetuses (unborn children in a late stage of development) that she could study. Abortions were illegal in Italy, so hospitals could not supply her with specimens. She knew that doctors or midwives willing to bend the law often performed these operations in secret, but she had no access to the results of them. All she had to work with was the occasional product of a miscarriage, or spontaneous abortion, usually obtained several days after the event and in poor condition. Not surprisingly, she did badly with the project, and Levi's scolding almost convinced her that she had no future as a laboratory scientist.

A sudden illness, resulting in an emergency operation, changed the relationship between Rita and her professor. Harsh though he could be, Levi cared deeply about his students. He visited Rita during her recovery and, when she returned to class after a monthlong absence, allowed her to drop the convolution project. After that time, Levi-Montalcini wrote, Giuseppe Levi became her mentor and friend. Like many of the professor's other interns, including Renato Dulbecco, she felt that Levi's enthusiasm when students did their work well more than balanced the criticism he could hand out so unsparingly when they did not meet his standards. Even that criticism itself, as Dulbecco later wrote, was educational:

Levi went into all the details of the work, examining all the results, and at the end he decided whether the result was good or not. I remember when he rejected some of my results. At first I was horrified, but once I thought it over, I came to recognize that Levi was right, and that his negative comments were in fact very useful for allowing me to make progress in my work. When Levi found that a result was interesting, he got very excited, and used to encourage us to continue in the direction he found interesting.

After Rita's recovery, Levi gave her and Eugenia a new assignment: finding out the roles that three types of tissue, the connective, muscular, and epithelial (tissue on the surface of the body), played in forming the weblike network of fibers (made of a protein called collagen) that supported them in the brain stem. Using an improved version of the silver stain created by Rita herself, the two young women showed for the first time that cells from all three types of tissue took part in creating the fibers. They used this research as the basis of their doctoral theses, which earned them top honors when they took their M.D. degrees in 1936. (As a reward for this achievement, Levi took the two young women to an international anatomy conference in Copenhagen, Denmark.)

Perhaps even more important, this assignment made Rita come to share Levi's greatest passion: investigation of nerve cells in tissue culture. Growing neurons in vitro—literally, "in glass," meaning in an artificial environment rather than in a living organism—had been possible only for about 20 years. Most biologists thought it unimportant, but Levi had realized that it gave scientists a chance to investigate the development of these vital cells while completely controlling their environment.

Most crucial of all, as Levi-Montalcini wrote, Levi's final project made her feel "passionate about research" for the first time. In doing so, it set up the shape of her future career.

Laboratory "à la Robinson Crusoe"

Anti-Semitism and political events may not have played much part in Rita Levi-Montalcini's waking life as she was growing up, but they did have a role in her nightmares. Her father had told her of the pogroms and other persecutions of Jews in Russia and Poland, as well as in Italy itself in earlier times, and she suggested in *In Praise of Imperfection* that she sometimes had dreams in which equally terrible things happened to her and her family.

Gathering Clouds

While Rita was still in high school, real-life nightmarish events began changing the political course of Italy. Like many other countries, Italy suffered economic unrest after World War I ended. Inflation

Benito Mussolini (1883–1945): Dictatorial "Leader"

Born in Predappio, near Forli, in the Romagna area of Italy on July 29, 1883, Benito Amilcare Andrea Mussolini was a Socialist in his youth. His father, a blacksmith, had been an active member of this political party as well. Mussolini became the editor of the official Socialist Party newspaper, *Avanti (Forward),* in 1912 and was a forceful labor leader in the city of Milan. He broke with the party in 1914, however, because he supported Italy's entry into World War I, whereas the Socialists opposed this move. Mussolini then founded a prowar group called Fasci d'Azione Rivoluzionaria and started his own newspaper, *Il Popolo d'Italia.* He served in the military beginning in 1915, but he was released in 1917 after being wounded during grenade practice.

During his Socialist years, Mussolini said that workers would have a better chance to seize power if they united into a tightly knit group, or *fascio.* This term came from *fasces,* the Latin word for a sheaf or bundle of grain in which all the stalks were tied together with a band. The *fasces* had been a political symbol since the days of ancient Rome, representing the idea that a closely united group was stronger than its individual members, just as the sheaf was sturdier than the individual grain stalks of which it was made. In March 1919, Mussolini formed a political movement called Fasci di Combattimento, which became a formal political party, the Partito Nazionale Fascista, in November 1921.

Mussolini's Fascist Party included a paramilitary group named the Blackshirts, which carried out vigilante actions against people whom the Fascists considered dangerous—including many of the Socialists who had formerly been Mussolini's comrades. By threatening that masses of Blackshirts would march on Rome in the fall of 1922 ("Either they give us the government or we shall take it," he told his throngs of supporters on October 24), Mussolini persuaded the Italian king Vittorio Emanuele III to make him the country's prime minister.

On January 3, 1925, Il Duce ("the leader"), as Mussolini's followers called him, announced that he was taking sole control of the Italian government. The king remained in office, but he was only a figurehead. Mussolini went on to disband opposition parties, parliamentary minorities, and the free press. He remained in power until he was finally overthrown in July 1943. Invading German armies made him the head of a puppet state in northern Italy after that, but

Benito Mussolini, shown here walking in Rome in 1936, was the founder of the Fascist Party and dictator of Italy from 1925 to 1943. (Associated Press)

Allied forces drove the Germans out two years later. Italian partisans (resistance fighters) captured Mussolini as he attempted to flee the country and executed him on April 28, 1945.

and other problems were not as severe there as in some other countries, such as Germany, but by 1920, some government officials were talking about the possibility of national bankruptcy. Workers occasionally staged violent demonstrations and often set up strikes. In Tuscany, for instance, 500,000 peasants went on strike during the summer of 1920, threatening the entire harvest of the area.

Upper-class and even middle-class Italians began to fear that Socialists and Communists, who supported such workers' rebellions, might disrupt the country or take their property away. After all, they pointed out, the Bolshevik Revolution, through which Communists had seized control of Russia in 1917, had, as Australian historian R. J. B. Bosworth later put it, "lurched into vicious civil war where sackings and massacre were everyday occurrences." Many Italians wanted a strong government that would control these apparently dangerous groups.

A man named Benito Mussolini offered such a government. In 1919 he and other veterans of World War I founded a revolutionary nationalistic group they called the Fasci di Combattimento (which later evolved into the Fascist Party). This party took increasing control of Italy during the early 1920s through a combination of propaganda and force. Mussolini became the dictator of Italy in 1925. The few people who dared to oppose Mussolini during his rise to power risked beatings or worse from gangs of thugs called the Blackshirts, a Fascist paramilitary group. For example, Giacomo Matteotti, a popular Socialist leader, disappeared in June 1924 and was later found to have been murdered by a Blackshirt named Amerigo Dumini. Mussolini almost surely knew about the murder before it occurred, and he may have ordered it. Widespread outrage greeted news of this crime—Levi-Montalcini remembered hearing her parents talking about it—but the protests were not strong or organized enough to shake Mussolini's hold on the government.

One person who spoke out against the Fascists was Levi-Montalcini's mentor, Giuseppe Levi. She and Levi's other students feared that his passionate, blunt remarks, spoken in public as often as in private "with supreme disdain for the most elementary rules of caution," would bring him to jail or worse. Although his respected position as head of the Institute of Anatomy usually kept him safe, he was arrested briefly after customs officers at the Swiss border caught his son Mario carrying anti-Fascist leaflets. Levi knew nothing about the plot that the Fascists said Mario was involved in, but he claimed all responsibility for it in the hope of protecting his son. He stopped his statements only after friends told him that Mario had escaped his captors by swimming across the freezing river that separated Italy from Switzerland. Levi was then released from jail.

When the Fascist government began requiring oaths of loyalty from college professors, Levi was torn. Swearing such an oath went against his personal principles, but he knew that failing to do so risked his position at the university and, with it, his chances of continuing his research and teaching. He therefore reluctantly took the oath.

Levi's speeches against the Fascist regime may have endangered him, but, at first, the fact that he was Jewish apparently did not. Unlike the Nazi Party, which took control of Germany in 1933, Mussolini's Fascists did not make anti-Semitism part of their official creed during their early years. Indeed, Mussolini said in 1934, "The Jews have lived in Rome since the days of Kings . . . [and] shall remain undisturbed." Il Duce himself had a Jewish mistress. In the mid-1930s, thousands of Jews fleeing Yugoslavia, Greece, and France after Nazi armies took over their homelands moved *into* Italy or Italian-controlled territories, seeing them as safe havens from the Germans.

At this same time, however, Mussolini's government was becoming more and more closely allied with the government of Germany. In a 1961 book *Storia degli ebrei italiani sotto il fascismo (The Jews in Fascist Italy: A History)*, respected Italian historian Renzo de Felice expressed the opinion that Mussolini began promoting anti-Semitism in Italy primarily as a kind of gift to Germany's leader, the violently anti-Jewish Adolf Hitler. For instance, Mussolini told his sister that the Fascists' attacks on Jews were merely "a showy but cheap token payment" to cement the ties between Italy and Germany. (This may not have been the whole story. Some later historians, such as Marie-Anne Matard-Bonucci, writing in 2007, have claimed that there was a strain of anti-Semitism in Italian fascism from the beginning.)

Rita Levi-Montalcini saw the first signs of Fascist anti-Semitism in events such as the group of arrests that followed Mario Levi's escape in 1934. Most of the people seized by the police were not just opponents of the Fascist Party, but Jews. Blatant propaganda attacks on Jews as a race did not begin until 1936, the year she graduated from medical school. During the next two years, increasing numbers of stories

Mussolini developed close ties with Germany in the 1930s. Many historians believe that Mussolini (left) began persecuting Italian Jews in order to impress Germany's powerful anti-Semitic leader, Adolf Hitler (right). (United States Holocaust Memorial Museum, courtesy Muzej Revolucije Narodnosti Jugoslavije)

blaming Jews for Italy's ongoing economic troubles or accusing them of other "crimes" appeared in Italian newspapers. Along with surprise, contempt, and predictable anger, Levi-Montalcini wrote later that she felt a kind of relief that "the monster of anti-Semitism . . . had come out of its lair" and made itself visible. The unfairness of the criticisms made her feel a new pride in being Jewish.

In the early days of the hate campaign, Levi-Montalcini was too wrapped up in her postgraduate studies to pay it much attention. Specializing in neurology and psychiatry, she treated patients at Turin's Clinic for Nervous and Mental Diseases. She also did laboratory work with another researcher, Fabio Visintini, to examine changes that took place in the appearance and activity of neurons in chicken embryos as the embryos developed. Chick embryos were popular tools for scientists studying the nervous system's development before birth because the unborn chick's nervous system is much simpler than that of fully developed birds or mammals—just a thousand or so cells, joined by a relatively small number of connections. At the same time, it is more complex and more similar to the system in humans than the nervous system of amphibians, which had been used for such experiments in the early part of the century.

Researchers in the early 20th century had discovered that nerve cells send a small electrical charge down the long fibers (called axons) that grow from them, and this charge is passed from cell to cell. Edgar Adrian, a British physiologist, had made the first electrical recordings from groups of nerve cells in 1925. More recently, an Australian researcher John Carew Eccles had developed electrodes small enough to penetrate the walls of nerve cells without destroying them. These electrodes allowed scientists to detect and record electrical signals from individual cells. In his experiments with Levi-Montalcini, Fabio Visintini recorded the electrical activity of the chick embryos' neurons, both the signals that the cells generated spontaneously and the ones they produced when stimulated through electrodes. Levi-Montalcini, meanwhile, used her version of the silver stain to bring out the physical changes that occurred in groups of neurons as they matured into their final form, or differentiated. Together the two researchers created a detailed, day-by-day picture of the changes that occurred as a chicken's nervous system developed.

The Racial Laws

The Fascists' anti-Semitic propaganda became harder to ignore after July 14, 1938, when Italian newspapers printed a statement by 10 so-called scientists. (Levi-Montalcini stated in her autobiography that only two of these had any real reputation, and both of them claimed later that the statement had misquoted them.) The "scientists" claimed that Jews should not be considered Italians at all: "They are made up of non-European racial elements that differ in absolute terms from the elements that are at the origins of the Italians." According to the historian of fascism Renzo de Felice, Mussolini himself edited parts of this racist manifesto.

Friends gathered around Levi-Montalcini, Giuseppe Levi, and other Jewish faculty members to offer sympathy, as they had after earlier attacks; Turin University had long been known as a stronghold of anti-Fascist sentiment. One young man, Germano, a friend of Levi-Montalcini's since medical school, even took the striking step of asking her to marry him. He was not Jewish, and he believed that marriage to him would protect her if anti-Jewish persecutions became more severe. Levi-Montalcini gently told him, however, that she had no wish to marry anyone.

Such a marriage soon would have become impossible, or at least illegal. On November 17, 1938, the Italian government issued a set of "Laws for the Defense of the Race" that forbade marriage between so-called Aryans and other races. More important to Levi-Montalcini, the new laws also banned Jews from all teaching jobs and most other kinds of work. As a result, she, her mentor, and many of the rest of Italy's 46,500 Jews found themselves suddenly unemployed.

Levi-Montalcini soon found a job outside of Italy. The director of the Neurologic Institute in Brussels, Belgium, offered her a research position there in March 1939. She was happy to accept, especially since her older sister, Nina, and Nina's family had already moved to Brussels. Giuseppe Levi took an academic position in another Belgian city, Liège, at about the same time, so Levi-Montalcini knew she would be able to visit him every weekend.

On September 12, 1939, while attending a research conference in Stockholm, Sweden, Levi-Montalcini heard the shocking news that Germany had invaded Poland. In essence, World War II had begun.

She quickly returned to Brussels, only to discover that the Belgians were deeply afraid that their country might be next on Hitler's list. Along with Nina's family, she drove across France in December to

As persecution of Jews increased in Italy in the late 1930s, the Fascist government sought to remove all traces of Jewish culture from the country. This photo shows the sign for a street in Milan whose name was changed in 1939 from Via Lazar Zamehof to Via Frecce Azzurre. (© Bettmann/CORBIS)

return to Italy. Most Italians had hoped that their country would stay out of any war that Hitler might start, but in May 1939, Mussolini had signed the so-called Pact of Steel, a military alliance with Germany that made Italy's involvement in such a war nearly unavoidable. Italy entered the war on the German side on June 10, 1940.

Levi-Montalcini's family now had a hard choice to make. They could emigrate to the United States, as a number of other Italian Jews, including Levi-Montalcini's old classmate Salvador Luria, had done, or to Argentina, like Levi-Montalcini's cousin Eugenia. (In his introduction to *Jews in Italy under Fascist and Nazi Rule, 1922–1945,* Joshua D. Zimmerman estimates that about 6,000 Italian Jews emigrated between the passing of the racial laws in 1938 and the German invasion of Italy in 1943.) Gino and Paola did not want to leave Italy, however; they felt sure that the Nazis and Fascists would soon be defeated. Wanting to minimize strain on their aging mother as well, the family decided to stay.

Levi-Montalcini, living in Turin once more with her mother, Paola, and Gino, found herself depressed and at loose ends. For a while, she continued to treat some of the people she had been caring for at the university clinic. She had to do so secretly, since practicing medicine was one of the many activities now forbidden to Jews. Her patients, most of whom were poor, were happy to have any doctor, Jewish or otherwise. Still, only non-Jewish physicians could prescribe drugs, and finding other doctors to write prescriptions for her became so difficult that after a few months Levi-Montalcini gave up her medical activities. After that, she had little to do except read and visit with friends.

Home Laboratory

In fall 1940, a meeting with an old acquaintance from Levi-Montalcini's student days, Giuseppe Levi's former star pupil, Rodolfo Amprino, opened up new possibilities for her. Recently returned to Italy from the United States, Amprino asked Levi-Montalcini about her current research projects. When she said she had none, he snapped, "One doesn't lose heart in the face of the first difficulties. Set up a small laboratory and take up your interrupted research." He

Rita Levi-Montalcini used chicken embryos because they were easy to obtain and to raise in her home laboratory. They are still a popular tool for research scientists, as this picture shows. (CDC/Dr. Stan Foster)

reminded her that Santiago Ramón y Cajal, the Spanish scientist who created the silver stain for nerve tissue that she used so often, had invented it with limited equipment in a small town.

Amprino's suggestion woke a spark in Levi-Montalcini, who (she wrote later) had always wished she could "undertake a voyage of adventure to unknown lands." The jungle she would explore on her journey, she decided, would be the billions of intertwined cells of the nervous system. She knew she could not continue the research she had been pursuing with Fabio Visintini, since she lacked both the equipment and the skill to make electrical recordings from nerve cells, but perhaps she could use her ability at performing microsurgery on chick embryos and applying the silver stain to their nervous tissue to carry out a different project. Chicken eggs, after all, were easy to obtain, and she could incubate them in a small space without complex equipment. Working around the racial laws would just make the challenge more exciting.

But what should she study? Seeking inspiration, Levi-Montalcini remembered an article she had read just a few months before while riding through the Italian countryside in an open cattle car with a friend. The government had commandeered all passenger trains to transport troops after war was declared, so civilians, if they traveled by train at all, had to make do with the bare floors of freight cars that had formerly been used to transport animals.

As she had sat on the edge of the car's platform on that summer day, with her legs dangling over the side and the smell of hay drifting in to her on the warm air, Levi-Montalcini leafed through a science magazine that Giuseppe Levi had given her two years before. She found herself focusing on an article written by Viktor Hamburger, a German-born scientist working in the United States. Like Levi-Montalcini, Hamburger was Jewish. He had come to the United States to do research in 1932 and, after realizing the threat to Jews that the Nazi takeover of Germany in 1933 represented, decided to stay. He had joined Washington University, in St. Louis, Missouri, in 1935 and become head of the university's zoology department in 1940.

Hamburger, too, had been investigating the development of the nervous system in chicken embryos. In 1934 he had found that when the developing wing of a three-day-old embryo was cut off before nerves reached it, the long fibers that had been growing toward the wing bud from the bodies of motor neurons in the spinal cord and nearby ganglia withered and died—and soon the neurons themselves died as well. (Motor neurons connect to muscles and give organisms the power to move.) Hamburger believed that the nerve cells died because they had been deprived of an unknown chemical that was produced by the nerve fibers reaching the wing. This chemical, he thought, traveled back along the fibers and signaled the central cells to mature and differentiate.

Now, looking for a project she could carry out in her home laboratory, Levi-Montalcini decided to repeat Hamburger's experiments and test his conclusions. She spent the rest of 1940 and early 1941 assembling the equipment she would need for what she had begun to think of as her "private laboratory à la Robinson Crusoe," which she would have to house in her bedroom. A box with a thermostat could serve as an incubator for her eggs. Another "hot box" allowed her to seal the chicken embryos in paraffin wax so that she could make thin slices of them for study on microscope slides. Gino built her a third box that could be kept at a constant temperature, with holes for her hands, in which she could operate on the tiny embryos while looking at them under a microscope.

Levi-Montalcini obtained miniature forceps (tweezers) from a watchmaker and microscissors from an eye doctor. With a fine-grained grindstone, she sharpened sewing needles to make tiny scalpels and spatulas. The only expensive equipment she had to buy were two microscopes, a stereomicroscope to use while operating on the embryos and a regular microscope with photographic equipment attached, which she needed to study and make a record of her stained preparations.

Surrounded as she was with news of war and German triumphs as Hitler's armies took over one European country after another, working on Hamburger's problem in her little laboratory "not unlike a convent cell" helped her keep at bay the fears that otherwise might have overwhelmed her, Levi-Montalcini wrote later. After removing limb buds from three-day-old embryos, she dissected a few embryos every six hours for the next 17 days. She made sections and stained slides from their spinal cords, which revealed the growth of neurons from the nearby ganglia. Unlike Hamburger, who had studied motor neurons, Levi-Montalcini focused on sensory neurons.

During some of her experiments, Levi-Montalcini had no less than Giuseppe Levi as her assistant. She had been very worried about the old professor during the first part of 1941. He had refused to leave Belgium even after Germany occupied it, and she had been afraid that the Germans might have captured him. However, he came back to Italy at the end of the summer. Levi-Montalcini asked him to advise her about her work, and, after that, he dropped by often to see her progress. Levi-Montalcini was always delighted to see him, even though his size and clumsiness cost her a certain amount of damaged slides and broken glassware.

Levi-Montalcini's work led her to some startling conclusions. To her eye, the silver-stained slices under her microscope revealed a different story from the one Hamburger had proposed. She saw that the nerve cells did differentiate after the wing was cut off—but then they died. She decided that the unknown chemical made in the wing bud attracted the nerve cells and encouraged their growth rather than making them differentiate. Without it, they could not survive.

She wrote a paper describing her experiments and, since no Italian scientific journal could publish the work of a Jewish researcher, sent it to a Belgian journal, *Archives de Biologie*, which eventually printed it. (A more extensive account was published in 1944 in the journal of the Italian Pontifica Academia Scientarum.) "It was a pure miracle that I succeeded with such primitive instrumentation," Levi-Montalcini said in *Nobel Prize Women in Science.*

In the Mountains

British planes began heavy bombing of Turin, a prime target because of its many industries, in summer 1942. Night after night the air-raid sirens wailed, and Levi-Montalcini and her family, like the other residents of the beleaguered city, retreated to their basements and prayed that the buildings above them would not be hit, potentially trapping them under the rubble. Just as some people carried family pictures or other small treasures with them for safekeeping, Levi-Montalcini brought her microscope and her best slides.

After a few months of these raids, Levi-Montalcini's family decided that the only safe thing to do was move out of Turin until the war was over. Many other Turinese were doing the same. The Levi-Montalcinis, now including Mariuccia, a young woman with whom Gino had recently fallen in love, rented a cottage in a hillside district called Asti, about an hour's bus or train ride from the city. Rita often returned to Turin in the daytime, when the city was safe.

By leaving Turin, the family may also have avoided the worst of a stepped-up Fascist campaign against the Jews. For instance, Gino, already a prominent architect, found himself listed next to Albert Einstein on an anti-Semitic poster urging that they and all other Jews be placed "up against the wall and then at them with a flame thrower!" Far from being frightened by this threat, however, Gino told the family that he was proud to be listed in Einstein's company. His lack of concern may have come partly from the fact that, according to both his sister and later historians, such verbal attacks were seldom followed up by actual violence.

In Asti, Levi-Montalcini's "Robinson Crusoe" laboratory was more cramped than ever—just a table in a corner of the family's living-dining room. Frequent cutoffs of electrical power added to her difficulties, and obtaining eggs became harder too. She had to ride her bicycle from one farm to another, begging for eggs for "her babies." She asked the farmers if they had roosters as well as hens, saying that she wanted fertilized eggs because they were "more nutritious." Thriftily, after she had extracted the embryos, she scrambled the eggs or made them into omelets for her family. This unnerved Gino so much when he found out that he thereafter refused to eat such dishes, even though he had been very fond of them before.

In spite of these increasingly challenging conditions, Levi-Montalcini went on with her work. (After she finished her research on the Hamburger problem, she went on to study nerves in the chick embryo's developing ear.) Over and over she saw files of nerve fibers leave their clusters of cells near the embryos' spines and—like ducklings following their mother, she wrote—migrate along the same paths to their final destinations in the chicks' bodies. Watching this process hour by hour, as though in a time-lapse film, she developed a new appreciation for the nervous system as a living, dynamic entity, changing constantly yet in a predictable way in response to changes in its environment. It reminded her of the changes she was seeing, also for the first time, in the plants and animals of the countryside as they responded to the warming days of spring. Similarly, she came to realize that, just as plants died in autumn and winter to make room for the new growth of spring, innumerable cells died in the course of even a normal, healthy embryo's development.

Meanwhile, in the world outside Levi-Montalcini's "convent cell," the war was going badly for Italy. Like Hitler, Mussolini had had grand dreams for his country: He had hoped to create a new Roman Empire and make the Mediterranean *mare nostrum,* "our sea," as it had been in ancient times. The Italian army, however, was not nearly as strong as he had believed. In April 1941, the Allies drove Italian soldiers out of northeastern Africa, part of which (Ethiopia) Italy had invaded in 1935. Allied troops invaded the Italian island of Sicily in July 1943, then moved into southern Italy in September. Meanwhile, increasing concern about wartime losses and dissatisfaction with Mussolini's other policies led to ever-stronger demands for Il Duce's resignation, and, on July 25, 1943, shortly after the invasion of Sicily, he was finally forced to submit it. He was arrested as he left the king's palace.

Levi-Montalcini's family heard the news on their radio that evening in Asti. The next morning, when Rita boarded the train into Turin, she found people laughing, crying, embracing one another, and throwing their Fascist badges in the air. She was happy to join in their rejoicing. The bad times were over at last—or so it seemed.

3

Years in Hiding

I n fact, for Rita Levi-Montalcini's family and the other Jews of Italy, the worst part of the nightmare was just beginning. German troops were already gathering on Italy's northern border when Mussolini resigned. On September 8, 1943—which started out as a happy time for the family because it was the day of Gino and Mariuccia's wedding—Pietro Badoglio, the new Italian prime minister, announced that the country was withdrawing from the war and surrendering to the Allies. The following day, as the Italian royal family and chief generals fled the country, German troops poured down from the Alps through the Brenner Pass and spread through northern Italy, unopposed by the remaining Italian troops. By September 10, Levi-Montalcini faced the grim sight of German tanks outside the Turin railway station.

Flight to Florence

Now Levi-Montalcini and her family realized—as, she wrote later, they probably should have done when Mussolini resigned in July—that, as Jews, they needed to flee the area immediately. "A delay of days, perhaps even of hours, might cost us our lives," Levi-Montalcini wrote in her autobiography. With the Germans in control, they knew that

✴ Dangerous Times: The Jews in Occupied Italy

Even after the Germans seized control of northern Italy, some Italian Jews still hoped that they would be relatively safe. "We thought that the position of the Jews in Italy was unique and that certain things could not happen here," an Italian witness said during Nazi Adolf Eichmann's trial for war crimes in 1961.

The Levi-Montalcini family was right not to be among these optimists. Meir Michaelis, a leading authority on the persecution of Jews in Italy during the German occupation, has stated that of about 45,000 Italian and foreign-born Jews in the country in September 1943, 7,682 died, most after being deported to German-run concentration camps outside the country. Of 8,369 Jews sent from Italy to such camps, only 979 returned.

Although some Fascists helped the Germans round up Italian Jews, many Italians, as the Levi-Montalcinis found out, risked their own safety to hide or otherwise protect their Jewish fellow citizens. At a ceremony in Rome on December 14, 1956, in which Italian Jews formally thanked the non-Jewish Italians who had helped them during the war, Sergio Piperno, the president of the Union of Jewish Communities, said:

> Everyone helped; all those who in some way could follow the moves of the occupying power and its collaborators were quick to warn their innocent and marked victims; all the friends, the acquaintances, the neighbors were quick to take them in, hide them and help them; everyone labored at procuring false documents for the Jews and derailing the searches.

Largely because of the Italians' courage, a higher percentage of Jews in Italy survived German occupation than in any other

captured Jews would most likely be either killed outright or sent out of the country to the Third Reich's concentration camps, where they would face Hitler's "final solution to the Jewish problem": death.

Levi-Montalcini wrote that her family had three choices, "each bristling with risk": to stay where they were and try to hide, to attempt to escape over the border into Switzerland, or to go south in the hope of encountering the British and Americans, who were

The Italian government drafted some Jews into forced labor, such as these workers shown in a lumber mill in Goriza in 1942. After German troops occupied northern Italy in the fall of 1943, however, Italian Jews risked a far worse fate: deportation to notorious German-controlled concentration camps such as Auschwitz. (United States Holocaust Memorial Museum, courtesy Marcello Morpurgo)

European country that fell under German rule except for Denmark. At Adolf Eichmann's trial for Nazi war crimes it was stated that "Every Italian Jew who survived [the occupation] owes his life to the Italians."

moving up the Italian peninsula. Their first choice was Switzerland, but, although Nina and her family eventually succeeded in sneaking across the border, the others gave up and turned back, deciding to try the southern option instead.

After the Germans marched into northern Italy, they freed Mussolini from his Italian prison and set him up as the head of a puppet state they called Repubblica Sociale Italiana (RSI), or the Italian Social Republic. It was often called the Republic of Salò, after the city on Lake Garda in which it had its headquarters. German troops began rounding up Jews in major Italian cities, including Rome, Genoa, Florence, and Milan. The Jews were sent to camps such as Fossoli and Bolzano, formerly internment camps for foreign-born Jews living in Italy, and from there they were deported to Auschwitz and other notorious German-run concentration camps outside of Italy.

All citizens had to carry identity cards, which German guards or soldiers could demand to see at any time. Jews, naturally, needed cards bearing false names and religions. Members of the Italian resistance movement, called the partisans, made many such cards as part of their underground war against the Fascists and the Germans. Fortunately, Rita and her family had been able to obtain some from a friend.

On October 7, 1943, the Levi-Montalcini family boarded a train heading south. The train, like all others, was packed with an assortment of civilian refugees and Italian ex-soldiers. The family had no idea what their final destination would be.

That decision was made for them when they ran into an old acquaintance of Rita's from her medical student days, now a Fascist officer, on the train. To Levi-Montalcini's horror, the man recognized her. When he asked where the group was going, Levi-Montalcini, fearing that he might alert the Germans to their presence, said hastily that they had boarded the train by mistake and were getting off at the next stop.

The next station proved to be in Florence. The Levi-Montalcini family stepped onto its platform at six in the morning in the pouring rain. Fortunately Paola had a friend in the city, and this friend, in turn, directed the group to a woman who was willing to rent them a

Rita Levi-Montalcini's family spent the years of the German occupation hiding in Florence, shown here. Many citizens of Florence, such as the Levi-Montalcinis' landlady, protected Jewish refugees. (Danilo Ascione, 2008, used under license from Shutterstock, Inc.)

room—provided that they were not Jews. The woman explained that she had nothing against Jews personally but did not want to take risks because she had to care for her sick father. The group showed her their false ID cards and assured her that they were Catholic. In fact, the family learned later, their new landlady guessed almost immediately that they were Jewish but was willing to help them anyway.

Life Underground

There was no question of Rita Levi-Montalcini doing research now, not even "à la Robinson Crusoe." She had had to leave her microscope and carefully prepared tools behind when the family fled Turin. Instead, she and Paola spent their days making false identity cards to give to other refugees who reached Florence and to the partisans. Levi-Montalcini wrote that the cards probably would not have stood up to even a moderately careful inspection, but they were better than nothing, and they gave the family a way to help others as they had been helped. She said she felt guilty later that she had not taken a larger part in resisting the Fascists and the Nazis, but she had feared endangering her family, especially her mother, and doubted that she would have had the "presence of mind" to stand up to Nazi interrogation and perhaps torture if she had been captured.

At night, with their radio's volume turned low to avoid detection, the family listened to news broadcasts from London and prayed that the Allies would take control of Italy soon. Meanwhile, the fearsome hunt for Jews went on in the streets around them. Iris Origo, an Anglo-American woman married to an Italian who was living in Florence at the time, wrote in her diary on November 28, 1943: "Last night they [the Germans] searched even the convents, hunting out and capturing the poor wretches who had taken refuge there including even a two-month-old baby deserted by its panic-stricken mother."

In spring 1944, Rita heard a familiar thunderous voice in her building's hallway: Giuseppe Levi, having narrowly escaped capture by the Germans while attempting to hide in the north, had arrived to rejoin his family, who, like the Levi-Montalcinis, were now living in Florence. He had the sense to ask the landlady only for "Rita," since he could not know what false last name his former student and her family were using, but then he spoiled the effect—not to mention putting his own life in danger—by announcing himself as "Professor Giuseppe Levi—ah, no, I keep forgetting, Professor Giuseppe Lovisato." During the next several months, Levi-Montalcini and Levi passed the time by editing a revised edition of Levi's two-volume textbook on histology.

On August 3, the German forces controlling Florence declared a state of emergency and shut the city down. Electricity and water were turned off. That night the townspeople watched in horror as troops blew up the bridges over the River Arno, many of which were architectural treasures hundreds of years old, to keep supplies from reaching the citizens.

Nonetheless, the tide began to turn against the Germans when the partisans started an organized rebellion in Florence on August 11. For several weeks, Rita and her mother and sister watched from their apartment as fighting raged in the streets below and Nazi snipers fired down from nearby rooftops. People dashed back and forth in spite of the risk, carrying household possessions with them as

The Partisans:
Italy's Resistance Movement

Many Italians, such as Giuseppe Levi, had opposed Italian fascism from the beginning—secretly or otherwise. The opposition movement became both more organized and, unavoidably, more hidden after the German invasion of northern Italy in September 1943. It was part of the resistance, the underground movement that fought the Nazis throughout Europe.

In Italy, the resisters were usually called partisans. They were a mixture of communists, socialists, liberals, and others who opposed Nazi and Fascist actions. Guido Boni, a close friend of Rita Levi-Montalcini's since her medical school days, was a member of one of the major partisan groups, the Partito di Azione (Action Party).

According to R. J. B. Bosworth's *Mussolini's Italy: Life Under the Fascist Dictatorship, 1915–1945*, there were about 200,000 Italian

(continues on next page)

Italian partisans, or resistance fighters, fought a guerrilla war against the Fascists and the Germans and helped Allied soldiers free Italy from German occupation. These partisans assisted South African troops entering Pistoia, 18 miles (30 km) from Florence, in December 1944. (Keystone/Hulton Archive/Getty Images)

(continued from previous page)

partisans in all. Unarmed citizens, including workers who staged strikes to slow the war effort and families who hid Jews, aided the efforts of the armed fighters among them or others threatened by the Germans. A massive partisan-led uprising on April 25, 1945, helped lead to the Germans' surrender of Italy to the Allies on May 2.

About 35,000 partisans were women. Some fought actively alongside the men. Others acted as *staffettas*, messengers carrying news and vital supplies between partisan groups. "A *staffetta* had to be ingenious in dealing with the unexpected," Maria de Blasio Wilhelm writes in *The Other Italy: The Italian Resistance in World War II*.

> She carried ammunition or parts of a printing press in an old shopping bag that appeared to be filled with worn-out clothing. She would casually push a baby carriage, its occupant reclining on hand grenades and bags of flour. "Pregnant" women concealed leaflets and contraband ID cards in skirts covering what appeared to be swollen bellies. A "Red Cross nurse" hurried along a country road, not to take care of a sick peasant but to take medical supplies to the partisans.

About 45,000 partisans lost their lives during the fighting or in concentration camps, and another 21,000 were wounded or disabled. Among those who survived the camps was famed Italian Jewish writer Primo Levi, like Rita Levi-Montalcini a native of Turin, who wrote movingly of his experience in Auschwitz, the death camp in Nazi-occupied Poland. Levi-Montalcini became a friend of Levi's and quoted his work at the end of her autobiography.

they fled from one part of the city to another. (The sight of these hurrying figures inspired Paola to paint what became one of her best-known works, *A Walking City*.) Frightening as the scene was, Levi-Montalcini wrote, it also stirred feelings of hope and brought "an exhilarating air of freedom": Help seemed to be on the way.

British troops seized control of Florence on September 2, 1944. Happily the Levi-Montalcinis threw away their false identity cards and took out cards bearing their real names, which they had brought with them and hidden.

The Refugees' Doctor

Knowing that physicians would be scarce, Levi-Montalcini immediately went to the Allied health service to volunteer. She and three other doctors, including Giuseppe Levi's son Alberto, were assigned to work in refugee camps that the health service had set up outside the city. Trucks full of peasant families, displaced from their homes by fighting in the Apennines south of Bologna, rumbled into these camps day and night.

Levi-Montalcini wrote that her service in the camps was her "most intense, most exhausting, and final experience as a medical doctor." She worked in a building complex that had once been a military barracks. Hundreds of refugees, sleeping on mattresses of straw, packed both the soldiers' dormitories and what once had been stables for their horses. As each new batch of exhausted people

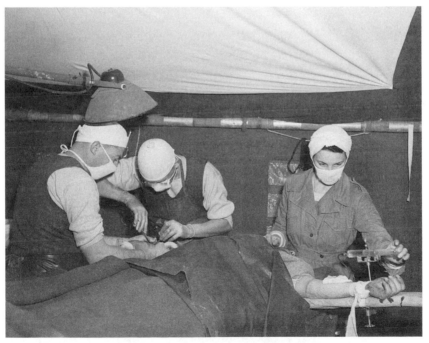

After Florence was freed and Rita Levi-Montalcini emerged from hiding, she worked as a volunteer physician at an Allied Health Service refugee camp for several months. This photo shows surgeons operating in a similar camp near the front lines of the U.S. Fifth Army in Italy in February 1944. (© Bettmann/CORBIS)

arrived, Levi-Montalcini checked them over and tried to find places for them to sleep. Many of the babies had been so weakened by cold, hunger, and thirst that they died soon after they arrived.

Crowded together as they were, refugee groups were easy prey for infections, which could quickly swell into epidemics as germs were passed from one person to another. During the chilly early months of 1945, an epidemic of abdominal typhoid, an often-fatal digestive illness caused by bacteria, struck Levi-Montalcini's camp. She learned later that the germs had been brought in through contaminated drinking water.

Antibiotics able to control the disease would arrive a mere few months later, but at the time, Levi-Montalcini had no effective medicine to offer. She was ordered merely to identify victims of the epidemic as quickly as possible and send them to the local hospital. Doctors there tried to treat the sick people by deliberately giving them fevers, which was thought to increase their bodies' resistance to the bacteria, but this treatment seldom worked, and many of the people died. This caused a problem for Levi-Montalcini because the refugees, who had welcomed and trusted her at first, began to fear being sent to the hospital so much that they hid from her examinations or lied to her about whether they were ill. She knew that her own life was also at risk during this time, perhaps even more so than it had been during the months in hiding, because she herself might contract the disease and die from it. She continued working for the health service until May 1945.

At last, on April 25, 1945, the Allies and their partisan supporters drove the Germans out of northern Italy, and the country was free once more. The Levi-Montalcinis returned to Turin in July to find the Turinese already hard at work rebuilding their damaged city. Giuseppe Levi also went home and took back his old position at the medical school. In turn, he restored Levi-Montalcini's job as his assistant, and she began a new research project with Rodolfo Amprino. Even though her life had returned to an appearance of normality, however, Levi-Montalcini had trouble recapturing the enthusiasm that had sustained her during the first part of the war.

In July 1946, Levi surprised Levi-Montalcini by calling her into his office. He had a letter for her, he said, from none other than

Viktor Hamburger, the scientist whose work she had duplicated— and questioned—in her "Robinson Crusoe" laboratory. Hamburger had read the paper describing her experiments, and he now invited her to come to Washington University and repeat the experiments with him. He thought that a stay of a semester or so would clear up the conflict between their results.

Levi-Montalcini was thrilled by the invitation. For one thing, she knew that being asked to work with Hamburger was a great honor. He was considered to be a founder of developmental neurobiology, or neuroembryology—the study of the nervous system's development before birth. He was the one who had made the chick embryo the standard research subject in this field. She also knew that Salvador Luria and some other scientists of her acquaintance had already emigrated to the United States and liked living there. (In fact, she learned later, Hamburger had consulted Luria about Levi-Montalcini before inviting her, and Luria had recommended her work.) She looked forward to a chance to be reunited with some of them and to see the country about which she had heard so much. She therefore thanked Hamburger for his offer and gladly accepted it. She had no idea that her "one-semester visit" would prove to last 30 years.

A Semester's Visit

Rita Levi-Montalcini did not travel to the United States alone. After returning to Turin, she had become reacquainted with Renato Dulbecco, whom she had known in medical school, and found that Dulbecco, like herself, felt at a loose end in his career. In spite of his medical degree, his real interest was in mathematics and physics.

Levi-Montalcini told Dulbecco that Salvador Luria was working at the University of Indiana at Bloomington in the rapidly expanding field of genetics. Like Dulbecco, Luria wanted to know how the laws of physics affect biological molecules, including the molecules of which genes are composed. Levi-Montalcini recommended that Dulbecco ask Luria, who by then was the chairman of the university's biology department, about the possibility of doing research with him in the United States. Dulbecco had an opportunity to do so when Luria visited Turin in the summer of 1946, and Luria offered him a fellowship.

Salvador Luria (1912–1991) and Renato Dulbecco (1914–): Genetics Pioneers

Salvador Luria and Renato Dulbecco, close friends of Rita Levi-Montalcini, had two important things in common with her. Both studied under Giuseppe Levi at the University of Turin's medical school, and both won Nobel Prizes in physiology or medicine. The two men also shared an interest in studying molecular biology, in which biology interacts with physics, and in examining the genes of viruses, the simplest known living things.

Born on August 13, 1912, in Turin, Luria graduated from medical school in 1935, a year ahead of Levi-Montalcini. In 1937, while studying radiology in Rome, he became inspired by the theories of Max Delbrück, a German-born physicist and pioneer of molecular biology then working at the California Institute of Technology (Caltech) in the United States. Delbrück urged scientists to think about genes as molecules, influenced by the same rules of physics and chemistry that affected other molecules. Following the advice

(continues on next page)

Salvador Luria was an old friend of Rita Levi-Montalcini's. He is shown here in 1969, the year he won the Nobel Prize in physiology or medicine for his work on the genetics of bacteria and viruses. (National Library of Medicine)

(continued from previous page)

of a friend (and, unknowingly at the time, Delbrück's lead as well), Luria began to study the genes of bacteriophages, a group of viruses that infect bacteria.

Failing to find work in Italy because of the Fascist government's increasingly repressive policies against Jews, Luria moved first to France in 1938 and then, when the Germans invaded that country in 1940, to the United States. He worked at a variety of universities, including the universities of Indiana (Bloomington) and Illinois (Urbana-Champaign) and the Massachusetts Institute of Technology. His research on bacteriophages led him to study the genetics of bacteria. His demonstration that bacteria developed resistance to viruses through genetic mutation, or natural alteration, helped to prove that bacteria had genes, which some researchers had doubted.

Luria also discovered that bacteria possessed chemicals that could protect them against bacteriophages by cutting the viruses' DNA (deoxyribonucleic acid, the material of which genes are made). These substances, called restriction enzymes, later became important tools of genetic engineering, helping scientists insert genes from one organism into the genome (complete collection of genes) of another. Luria shared the 1969 Nobel Prize in physiology or medicine with Delbrück and another bacteriophage researcher, Alfred Day Hershey. Luria died of a heart attack on February 6, 1991.

Renato Dulbecco was born in Catanzaro, Italy, on February 22, 1914. He graduated from medical school in the same year as Levi-Montalcini, even though he was five years younger. During the German occupation of Italy he served as a physician to a partisan group.

Dulbecco worked with Luria in Indiana for two years, then moved to Caltech to collaborate with Max Delbrück, whom he had met through Luria. Dulbecco studied bacteriophages for several years, then began examining viruses that infect animals. He and his students demonstrated that some viruses caused cancer in animals by inserting certain genes into the genomes of the cells they infected. One of these students, Howard Temin, and another researcher named David Baltimore went on to discover reverse transcriptase, the enzyme that allows the viruses to perform this feat. Dulbecco, Temin, and Baltimore shared the Nobel Prize in physiology or medicine in 1975 for their discoveries. At the Salk Institute in La Jolla, California, of which he was president from 1988 to 1992, Dulbecco continued to study the genetics of cancer until his retirement in 1992.

A Fresh Start

Rita Levi-Montalcini and Renato Dulbecco boarded the Polish ship *Sobieski* in Genoa on September 19, 1946, and set sail for New York. On their arrival, they gaped at the Statue of Liberty in the harbor as the public-address system warned everyone not to crowd on the same side of the ship in their eagerness to spot the famous landmark. Like other immigrants, they waded through the battery of questions and examination of papers at the immigration service desk. Then, finally, they were free to go. Dulbecco went on to Bloomington, while Levi-Montalcini spent two days with cousins who lived in New Jersey, visiting such well-known sights as New York City's Empire State Building. She then climbed aboard a luxury train bound for St. Louis.

St. Louis boasted about 2 million people at the time of Levi-Montalcini's arrival. It had been the site of the 1904 World's Fair, also called the Louisiana Purchase Exposition, and many structures from the fair remained. Earlier still, the city, located on the Mississippi River, had been famous as the "gateway" to the country's western expansion by land, the starting point for wagon trains that carried settlers across prairies and deserts to their new homes in the mid-1800s. St. Louis seemed an appropriate place for Levi-Montalcini to begin a new phase in her career. "I felt at home the day I landed" in the city, a 2003 article in the *St. Louis Post-Dispatch* quoted her as saying.

Washington University, founded in 1853, was on the west side of the city. Levi-Montalcini was pleased at

Renato Dulbecco, shown here in 1966, came to the United States with Rita Levi-Montalcini in 1946. Like Levi-Montalcini and Salvador Luria, Dulbecco won a Nobel Prize in physiology or medicine (in 1975). His prize was awarded for his study of viruses, including viruses that can cause cancer. (National Library of Medicine)

Rita Levi-Montalcini began working with Viktor Hamburger at the Washington University School of Medicine in 1946 and remained associated with the school until her retirement in 1977. This photograph shows the university's modern medical center, including the School of Medicine. (Washington University School of Medicine)

the sight of its ivy-covered brick buildings but startled at the informality of the students lounging on the grass around them, so different from the reserved behavior she was used to seeing at the university in Turin. (When she later observed students relaxing in the library with their feet on the tables, she imagined the roar that Giuseppe Levi would have given if he had beheld such a thing!) The university's peaceful atmosphere, Levi-Montalcini wrote in an autobiographical sketch in *Women Scientists: The Road to Liberation,* seemed to her like "the garden of Eden."

Viktor Hamburger was waiting for Levi-Montalcini in the zoology department library. She liked the white-haired Hamburger at once, as did most of the people who met him throughout his career. A biographical sketch of Hamburger published online by the Society for Developmental Biology states that Hamburger "touched all who knew him by his wisdom, dignity, generosity, and kindness." Hamburger, for his part, saw an uncertain young woman who, Sharon McGrayne quotes him as saying, "was very humble and modest." Levi-Montalcini knew little English at the time and, he said, for the first two years of her stay in the United States "felt very awkward."

On that first day, Hamburger invited Levi-Montalcini to have dinner with himself and his wife, Martha, at their home. After the meal concluded, he took her to meet a middle-aged couple who had agreed to rent her a room. Perhaps not realizing that Levi-Montalcini was Jewish, her new landlady wasted no time in offering her opinions about politics and religion, which included a strong dislike of Jews. Not surprisingly, Levi-Montalcini made different, and happier, rooming arrangements a week later. (She also encountered some anti-Semitism within St. Louis's tight-knit Italian immigrant community, she wrote later, though she made some new friends there as well.)

Two Fields Converge

Viktor Hamburger thought that his background and Rita Levi-Montalcini's complemented each other. "I came from experimental and analytical embryology, of which Rita hadn't the foggiest idea," he stated in *Nobel Prize Women in Science.* "Rita . . . knew the nervous system, of which I had only the foggiest idea." Both of these fields had come into existence only in the late 19th century, when microscopes improved enough to make body cells and the detailed structure of tissues dependably visible for the first time.

Before modern compound microscopes were invented, philosophers and scientists had argued endlessly about how new lives began. They knew that most living things were born from the union of a male and a female, but no one was sure what each sex contributed.

Rita Levi-Montalcini came to Washington University to study with eminent neuroembryologist Viktor Hamburger, shown here in 1987. Hamburger's research laid the groundwork for Levi-Montalcini's later discoveries. (WU Photographic Services Collection, University Archives, Department of Special Collections, Washington University Libraries)

Researchers also disagreed about the way development occurred. Some thought that living things existed in miniature form in the male or female sex cells and simply grew larger as the embryos developed. (A few scientists even claimed to have seen microscopic human forms inside sperm cells.) Others thought that organisms formed first in a very simple state and grew more complex as they matured.

The picture of development became clearer after microscopes improved. Scientists learned that most living things began as a single cell, the fertilized egg, which was created when a sex cell from a female (an egg cell) fused with a sex cell from a male of the same species (a sperm cell). They showed that development proceeded from a small and simple form, in which all the cells were essentially alike, to a larger and more complex one, in which the cells had differentiated into the many types of tissues and organs that make up a complete plant or animal.

The study of the processes of development, especially development before birth, became known as embryology. (Today, this field is called developmental biology and covers all stages of development, both before and after birth.) In the early 20th century, researchers began to have the power to examine these processes in more detail and perform experiments to test ideas about them. For instance, they cut developing limbs off amphibian or, later, chick embryos or grafted extra limbs onto them and observed what happened to the rest of the embryos' bodies.

Scientists wanted to know what guided the many changes involved in embryonic development. Hans Spemann, a German researcher, found one answer to this question in 1924. Spemann and coworker Hilde Mangold discovered that a certain part of an amphibian embryo, when transplanted into earlier, formless embryos, could make those embryos take on more developed characteristics. Spemann called this special tissue the "organizer" and referred to its effects on the formless tissue as induction. Different parts of the organizer induced formation of different tissues and organs: One end produced parts of the head, for instance, while the other end produced parts of the tail. As tissues developed, they in turn had inductive (secondary organizer) effects on later-developing tissues and organs. Spemann was awarded a Nobel Prize in physiology or medicine in 1935 for his discovery of organizers.

Viktor Hamburger had been a student of Spemann's at the University of Freiburg during the years when the organizer was discovered. Much of Hamburger's work, including the experiments that Rita Levi-Montalcini duplicated in her "Robinson Crusoe laboratory," applied Spemann's ideas about induction and organizers to the formation and development of the nervous system.

Levi-Montalcini's field, neurobiology, was only a little older than Hamburger's. Nerve cells became clearly visible under the microscope for the first time around 1873, when an Italian scientist, Camillo Golgi, invented a silver-containing stain that neurons absorbed but the cells around them did not. Slides of nerve tissue stained in this way showed the nerve cells as black or dark gray against a yellow background of supporting cells. A second pioneer neuroanatomist, Spanish scientist Santiago Ramón y Cajal, improved this stain and created others in the early 1900s. Using and expanding on these two experts' techniques, researchers examined the nerve cell bodies and the single long fiber that extended from each one. They also observed many shorter, thinner fibers growing out of the cells, which were termed dendrites because they looked like the branches of trees (*dendron* is the Greek word for *tree*). Especially in the brain and spinal cord, researchers saw nerve cells and their fibers forming dense webs of connections with one another.

Santiago Ramón y Cajal carried out the first studies of the nervous system's development before birth. As Viktor Hamburger and Rita Levi-Montalcini later would do, Ramón y Cajal used chick embryos in early stages of development as his experimental subjects. Chick neurons were very similar to those of humans and other mammals, he observed, and they took up the silver stain exceptionally well. Ramón y Cajal found that the nervous system in these embryos developed according to such a predictable pattern that a trained researcher looking at a slide of the system could immediately tell the age of the embryo from which it came.

Understanding the way the nervous system functioned proved to be even harder than understanding its structure. Golgi and Ramón y Cajal disagreed about whether the nervous system was organized, and should be studied, cell by cell or as a single network of fibers that could not be subdivided. Ramón y Cajal proposed the cell-by-cell theory, while Golgi supported the network theory. This disagreement erupted into a public argument between the two men, sparked by comments in Golgi's acceptance speech, when both went to Sweden in 1906 to receive shares of that year's Nobel Prize in physiology or medicine. By Levi-Montalcini's time, electron microscopes had revealed tiny gaps called synapses between connecting neurons, leading most scientists to adopt the cell-by-cell approach, but she met a few researchers who still held onto the network theory.

Scientists discovered that nerve cells send a small electrical charge down their axons, and this charge is passed from cell to cell. (Levi-Montalcini had learned about these electrical charges during her postdoctoral work with Fabio Visintini in Turin in the late 1930s.) They also learned that neurons release chemicals called neurotransmitters, which are taken up by nearby nerve cells. Scientists in the 1930s and early 1940s disagreed about whether the electrical or the chemical exchange was more important in passing signals from one neuron to the next—a dispute Levi-Montalcini described in her autobiography as "the battle between the soup and the spark." By the late 1940s, both had been shown to be important: Electric current carried signals down nerve cells' fibrous axons from the cell bodies, but neurotransmitters brought the signals across the synapses from the axon of one cell to the dendrites and cell body of another.

Embryology and neurobiology, the two lines of research to which Hamburger and Levi-Montalcini were heirs, came together in the work of Paul Weiss, an Austrian researcher who moved to the United States in 1931. In the 1930s, Weiss tried to discover how nerves from the brain and spinal cord grow into limbs or other organs on the edges, or periphery, of the body during embryonic development. Some researchers thought that a preexisting, unchangeable program determined the pattern of such growth—the sort of thing that later scientists would say was controlled by genes. Others, following Hans Spemann's "induction" ideas, thought that the organs themselves guided the nerves in some way. According to this theory, changing the organs, for instance adding or removing a limb, would change the pattern of nerve growth.

The Synapse

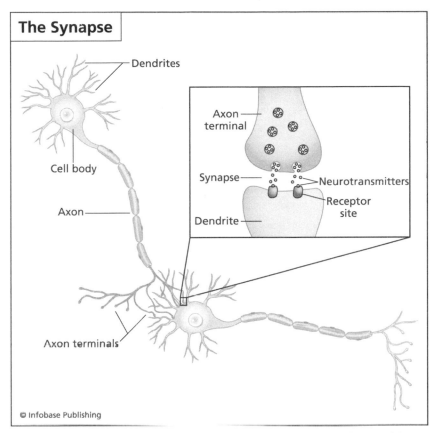

Dendrites

Cell body

Axon

Axon terminals

Axon terminal

Synapse

Dendrite

Neurotransmitters

Receptor site

© Infobase Publishing

By the time Rita Levi-Montalcini came to Washington University, researchers studying the nervous system had learned that nerve cells send messages to one another across gaps called synapses. The signal transmission is both electrical and chemical. An electrical impulse travels down a nerve cell's long central fiber, or axon. When the signal reaches the end of the axon, it causes the formation of small bodies (vesicles) that contain biochemicals called neurotransmitters. The vesicles release the neurotransmitter molecules through the cell membrane into the synapse. The molecules then travel across the synapse to the membrane of a short fiber (dendrite) of a neighboring cell. They attach themselves to receptor molecules on the surface of that cell and generate another electrical signal, which travels through the second cell.

Grafting extra limb muscles onto amphibians, Weiss obtained results that he believed supported the induction theory. However, one of Weiss's pupils, Roger Sperry, challenged this idea in the late 1930s. Sperry used surgery to switch nerves in rats and other mammals, for instance moving a nerve from a muscle that flexed (flexor) to a muscle that functioned by extending (extensor) instead, and vice

Viktor Hamburger and other neuroembryologists studied the development of the nervous system by observing how limbs developed in normal chick embryos, such as this nine-day-old specimen, and by seeing what happened when they made experimental changes, such as grafting extra limbs onto an embryo or removing normal limbs. (© Peter Arnold, Inc./Alamy)

versa. He also cut the optic nerves of salamanders, a type of amphibian, and then removed the animals' eyes and reimplanted them upside down, after which the optic nerves regenerated. (Unlike mammals, amphibians can regrow damaged parts of their bodies.) In contrast to Weiss, Sperry found that in both the rats and the salamanders, the nerves' functions remained the same no matter where the nerves were placed. This result strongly supported the idea of "hard-wired" genetic preprogramming. Levi-Montalcini met both Sperry and Weiss at a neurobiology conference in Chicago in March 1949.

Hamburger's early research, on determining how grafting or removing limbs on chick embryos affected the growth of nerves going from the spinal cord to the limbs, followed up the work of Weiss and Sperry. It was some of this research that had inspired Levi-Montalcini, after she read about it while riding in the cattle car on that summer day in 1940, to set up her makeshift home laboratory. Now, in 1947 and 1948, she was having the chance to duplicate her work with the master himself.

An End to Discouragement

Busy as she was on her research with Viktor Hamburger, Rita Levi-Montalcini found time during the early months of her stay in St. Louis to travel around the city and enjoy it as a visitor. She admired the classic architecture of the old buildings downtown, took Sunday trips down the Mississippi River on a passenger boat called the *Admiral,* and picnicked with other department members on small boats traveling the lakes and rivers that ran through the Ozark Mountains.

Levi-Montalcini also visited Salvador Luria and Renato Dulbecco in Bloomington, relishing the opportunity to talk about their research and her own. She envied them the excitement in the field of genetics. She felt that recent advances in that field were giving it a precision that her own specialty did not have.

When Levi-Montalcini was at Bloomington, Luria and Dulbecco introduced her to several stars of genetic research. One was Hermann Müller, who had just (in October 1946) won the Nobel Prize in physiology or medicine for studies showing how radiation increased the number of mutations, or genetic alterations, in fruit flies. Müller had also been one of the first to suggest approaching genetics through the study of viruses. To Levi-Montalcini, people like Müller represented, as she put it, "Science with a capital *S.*"

Luria also introduced Levi-Montalcini to (he said) his own brightest student, a gawky young man named James Watson. Luria's high opinion of Watson proved to be prophetic. A few years later, in 1953, Watson and British scientist Francis Crick, working at Britain's Cambridge University, figured out the structure of the DNA molecule, thereby revealing how the molecule could reproduce itself and opening a new era in genetics. Watson and Crick, too, earned shares of a Nobel Prize in physiology or medicine (in 1962, with Maurice Wilkins). Watson came to have a reputation for disregarding women scientists, such as British chemist Rosalind Franklin, whose X-ray photographs of DNA, "borrowed" without her knowledge, helped him and Crick make their discovery. Levi-Montalcini reported in her autobiography that Watson, true to form even at this early stage in his career, "took no interest in me whatsoever" at their meeting.

During the first months of her research with Hamburger, Levi-Montalcini repeated the work that she had done in her "Robinson

Crusoe" laboratory. The results convinced Hamburger that her interpretation of the research had been the correct one. Hamburger, in fact, was so impressed with Levi-Montalcini's performance that he extended the time of her appointment at the university and offered her the position of research associate.

Nonetheless, Levi-Montalcini felt discouraged. The fields in which she was working, experimental embryology and experimental

Genetics: The Roots of Inheritance

Just as humans had always wondered how new organisms developed, they had wondered how traits, or characteristics, were inherited within families. The first person to discover a clue to this riddle was Gregor Mendel, a 19th-century Austrian monk. Working in his monastery garden, Mendel bred peas that had different features, such as green or yellow pods. He carefully observed and counted hundreds of plants, then wrote a paper describing simple mathematical rules that determined which of two competing characteristics an offspring plant was likely to inherit. These traits were passed on through what Mendel called "factors." He had no idea what these factors were, physically, but he wrote that an offspring received two sets of them, one from its female parent and one from its male parent.

Mendel's paper was published in 1866, but for 34 years, almost no one read it. Then, in 1900, three scientists independently rediscovered Mendel's work and republished it. A fourth scientist, William Bateson, pointed out that Mendel's rules could provide the mechanism behind Charles Darwin's theory of evolution through natural selection, which by then was coming to be widely accepted. In 1909, Bateson founded a new scientific field that he called genetics. Another researcher, Wilhelm Johansson, shortly afterward suggested substituting the word *gene* for Mendel's *factor* as the unit of genetics—the carrier of a single inherited trait.

In the early 20th century, Walter Sutton, an American, and Theodor Boveri, a German, suggested independently that genes were part of wormlike bodies called chromosomes, located in the central body, or nucleus, of most cells. Most body cells contained multiple pairs of chromosomes, but sex cells—the cells that grew into sperm and egg cells—have only one chromosome from each pair. When an egg and a sperm cell unite to begin a new organism,

neurobiology, lacked the equivalent of the new tools that were aiding her friends' research in genetics. She wondered if scientists knew— or perhaps ever would know—enough about the developing embryo and the nervous system to be able to investigate them systematically. She confided her concerns to Luria during her visits to Bloomington. He was unable to reassure her, but he advised her to go on with her studies in spite of her doubts.

the resulting fertilized egg again acquires pairs of chromosomes, with one member of each pair coming from the father and one from the mother. Thomas Hunt Morgan's research group at Columbia University in New York City used fruit flies to prove the chromosome theory and trace the genes for certain inherited traits to parts of particular chromosomes.

Researchers still did not know what genes really were, however. Chromosomes, they found, were made up of two kinds of biochemicals: proteins, the large class of compounds that does most of the work in cells, and nucleic acids, more mysterious substances first discovered in 1869. Most geneticists assumed that genes were made of proteins, which were known to be quite complex. In 1944, however, Oswald Avery and his coworkers at New York's Rockefeller Institute for Medical Research (later Rockefeller University) showed that purified deoxyribonucleic acid (DNA), a type of nucleic acid, from bacteria could change traits in other bacteria, and this change could be inherited. Avery's experiment convinced many geneticists that genes must be made of DNA rather than protein.

Salvador Luria, Renato Dulbecco, and others in the forefront of genetic research studied bacteriophages and other viruses because they saw these microorganisms as what James Watson and Andrew Berry's history of modern genetics, *DNA: The Secret of Life*, calls "naked genes." Their research was beginning to reveal how viruses passed on genetic information to cells they infected and how bacteria, in turn, passed on traits that allowed them to resist the viruses. Although Rita Levi-Montalcini knew little about genetics in the 1940s, she could see that genetic programming was bound to have a major influence on her own area of study, the development of the embryonic nervous system.

Structure of DNA

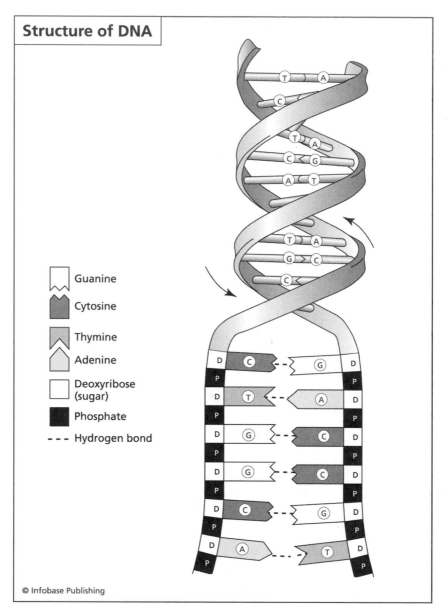

Guanine

Cytosine

Thymine

Adenine

Deoxyribose (sugar)

Phosphate

- - - Hydrogen bond

© Infobase Publishing

James Watson and Francis Crick deduced in 1953 that each molecule of deoxyribonucleic acid (DNA) is made up of two coiled "backbones" composed of alternating smaller molecules of phosphate (P) and deoxyribose (D), a sugar. Inside the backbones, like rungs on a ladder, are four kinds of smaller molecules called bases: adenosine (A), thymine (T), cytosine (C), and guanine (G). When the DNA molecule reproduces, the hydrogen bonds holding the pairs of bases together come apart, and each strand of the molecule forms a new complementary strand, creating two identical molecules.

Fortunately, Levi-Montalcini's concerns about the future of her research did not last long. One day in fall 1947, she was looking at a group of slides she had made of chick embryos between the third and seventh day of development, when neurons in the birds' brains and spinal cords were just beginning to form. She had done a particularly good job of staining the nerve cells, so they showed clearly against the background of other cells. She saw that this stage of development seemed to be an exceptionally dynamic one in certain parts of the spinal cord, with striking changes taking place over just a day or even a few hours.

In two areas of the cord, Levi-Montalcini saw thousands of neurons streaming in long lines from one place to another, making her think of "the maneuvers of large armies on a battlefield." At a different spot, by contrast, she saw masses of nerve cells showing changes that meant they were dying. Continuing her war metaphor, she wrote in her autobiography that this scene was like "a battlefield covered with corpses." At a slightly later stage of development, she witnessed bloblike macrophages, "scavenger" cells from the immune system (the body's defense system), cleaning up the "battlefield" by devouring the remains of the dead neurons. Levi-Montalcini saw this pattern repeat in slide after slide made from different embryos, strongly suggesting that a genetic program was guiding this part of the nervous system's development.

For Levi-Montalcini on that day, "nerve cells were acquiring a personality not usually attributed to them." She had never been so aware that the nervous system was constantly changing. Also, although she had noticed cells dying in the embryos she had studied in Asti in the spring of 1943, she had never been so struck by the fact that cell death and migration as well as growth and differentiation were part of the system's normal development. She knew that this idea was a new one in science. Her intuition, which she had come to value highly, told her that investigating these processes might provide a novel and important way to understand the nervous system.

"Intoxicated" by her discoveries, Levi-Montalcini hurried to Viktor Hamburger's office. She brought him back to her laboratory and showed him slides and sketches of what she had seen. He, too, became excited, believing that she had indeed found a new key to studying the nervous system's development. After he left, Levi-Montalcini, who had put a record player in her laboratory, celebrated by playing one of her favorite records, a Bach cantata. To her, this thrilling day marked not only the end of her doubts about neuroembryology but "the sealing of a lifelong alliance between me and the nervous system, an alliance I have never broken or regretted keeping."

5

Halo of Nerves

R ita Levi-Montalcini's research took a new direction in January
1950, when Viktor Hamburger showed her a 1948 journal
article written by Elmer Bueker, a former pupil of Hamburger's
then working at Georgetown University, in Washington, D.C. Like
Hamburger and Levi-Montalcini, Bueker was trying to find out how
the development and differentiation of the chick embryo's nervous
system were regulated. Following up on an idea that Hamburger
had suggested, Bueker had transplanted tiny pieces of cancerous
tumors onto embryos instead of grafting extra limbs onto them.
He wanted to see how the embryos and the transplanted tumors
affected one another. Both tumors and embryo limb buds were fast-
growing tissues, so he and Hamburger thought that their effects on
the embryo might be similar.

Puzzling Experiments

One of the tumors Bueker used, a mouse cancer called S.180, produced startling results. Three to five days after the tumors began to grow on three-day-old chick embryos, fibers from neurons in the embryos' sensory ganglia extended themselves into the tumors, just as they would have done into transplanted limbs—but even more vigorously. (Sensory neurons detect information from the environment and convey it to the brain.) Bueker suspected that something in the tumor cells was stimulating the sensory cells' growth. He thought the growth was greater than growth into a transplanted limb would have been because the tumor provided a larger area for the cells to expand into than a limb would have.

Both Hamburger and Levi-Montalcini were intrigued by Bueker's report. They decided that Levi-Montalcini should stop her current work and try to repeat Bueker's experiment in the hope of understanding it better.

Levi-Montalcini obtained mice with S.180 tumors and transplanted limb-sized pieces of the tumors onto chick embryos. The cancer cells soon formed a mass on one side of each embryo. When Levi-Montalcini examined slides made after the tumors were well established, she saw what she called (in her autobiography) "an extraordinary spectacle." Nerve fibers did not simply grow into particular parts of each tumor, as they would have into a grafted limb. Instead, bundles of fibers grew everywhere among the cells, "like rivulets of water flowing steadily over a bed of stones." Equally strangely, the fibers failed to connect with any of the cells, though they would have formed such connections in a limb.

That was just the beginning of the surprises. Most of the fibers, Levi-Montalcini saw, did not come from the sensory ganglia, as had happened in Bueker's experiments. Instead, the fibers grew out of cells in the sympathetic ganglia, which supply nerves that control automatic reactions such as heartbeat and blood flow. These ganglia also cluster along the spinal cord. Bueker had reported that the sensory ganglia in his embryos had grown larger on the side of each embryo that was closer to the transplanted tumor tissue, and Levi-Montalcini saw this effect as well. Like the overall growth, it was even more striking in the sympathetic ganglia than it was in the sensory ones.

Levi-Montalcini felt that the nerve growth produced by the mouse tumor tissue was quite different from the growth that transplanting extra limbs onto an embryo stimulated: It was something entirely new. This feeling was confirmed one day in fall 1950 when she looked at the results of similar experiments she had done with another mouse tumor, S.37. Like S.180, this tumor was a sarcoma, or cancer originating in connective tissue, that had originally come from the mammary gland (breast). It, too, grew vigorously when grafted onto the chick embryos. The slides Levi-Montalcini was examining had been made from embryos that were 11 days old, eight days after the tumors had been transplanted onto them.

The webs of sprouting nerve fibers on the slides appeared so thick that, as she stared at them, Levi-Montalcini thought that "I might be hallucinating." All the sympathetic ganglia along the spinal cord were enlarged, not just the ones nearest to or in contact with the tumor tissue. The fibers sprouting from them, furthermore, grew not only into the tumors but also into all the surrounding parts of the embryo, which normally would not yet contain nerves. The dots of tissue that would later become kidneys, liver, thyroid, and sexual organs—all were packed with nerve fibers, none of which made any connection with the cells they wove among. "These findings demonstrated that the tumor promoted an excessive growth of the sympathetic system with total disregard for the requirements of the organism, altering the sequence of events which characterize normal developmental processes," Levi-Montalcini wrote in *The Saga of the Nerve Growth Factor,* a collection of pioneering papers by herself and others. "The sympathetic system overtook . . . [all] other embryonic organs and tissues."

The fibers had even formed clumps inside the embryo's veins— something Levi-Montalcini had never seen before. They had not penetrated the other type of blood vessel, the arteries, however. This difference was important, Levi-Montalcini realized: Veins would carry substances from the tumor into the embryo, whereas blood in the arteries flowed the other way. Levi-Montalcini concluded that the tumors must release some liquid compound that stimulated the growth and differentiation of nerves, especially sympathetic nerves. "This hypothesis . . . became a certitude with me long before I obtained supporting evidence in its favor," Levi-Montalcini wrote in *The Saga of the Nerve Growth Factor.*

The fact that the fibers had grown into the veins, furthermore, suggested to Levi-Montalcini that the mystery substance not only

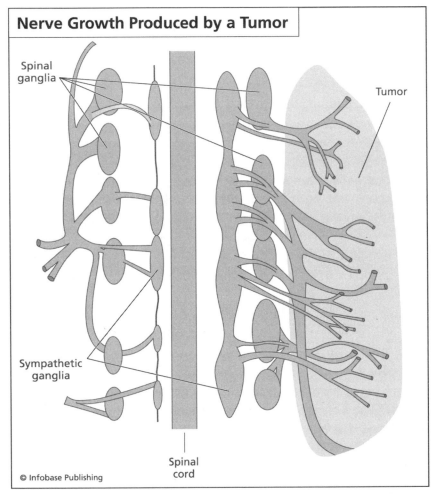

Nerve Growth Produced by a Tumor

Spinal ganglia

Tumor

Sympathetic ganglia

Spinal cord

© Infobase Publishing

The nerve growth that certain mouse tumors stimulated when grafted onto chick embryos was so amazing that when Rita Levi-Montalcini first saw it in 1950, she "thought [she] might be hallucinating." Nerve fibers growing from the embryo ran everywhere among the tumor cells "like rivulets of water flowing . . . over a bed of stones," yet they did not contact the cells, as they would have done if growing into a normal limb. The nerve fibers even formed clumps inside the veins that ran through the tumor tissue, but they did not penetrate the tumor's arteries. This behavior suggested to Levi-Montalcini that the nerves were being stimulated by a liquid created in the tumor.

made nerves grow but attracted them to itself. A biomolecule that had both these powers would indeed be revolutionary. Yet, amazed and excited as she was by the unknown compound's possibilities, Levi-Montalcini wrote in *In Praise of Imperfection* that "the new field of research that was opening before my eyes was, in reality, much vaster than I could possibly have imagined."

Convincing Evidence

During the next few months, Levi-Montalcini tested a variety of tumors in her chick embryo system. Many of the cancers grew on the embryos, but only the two breast sarcomas had any effect on the embryos' nerve tissue. Those, on the other hand, produced a startling growth of nerves every time she tested them.

While Levi-Montalcini was carrying out this work, she was startled one morning to hear a familiar voice "thundering" in the hallway: Giuseppe Levi had come to see her. She had heard that he was planning to visit the United States, but she had not known that he would reach St. Louis. Levi was still as vigorous and red-haired as ever in spite of being in his 80s. Eagerly, Levi-Montalcini showed her old mentor her slides and drawings, expecting his praise.

To Levi-Montalcini's horror, Levi let out the sort of roar that she remembered all too vividly from her medical school days. If she published this work, he shouted, she would ruin her reputation and perhaps even his. The fibers she was seeing, he insisted, were not nerves at all but simply connective tissue. Hadn't she learned *anything* in all those years with him?

Levi-Montalcini felt sure that, for once, her former teacher was wrong, but she did not know how to prove it to him. With a cleverness born of desperation, she changed the subject by asking him whether he had seen the Grand Canyon yet. Perhaps, now that he was not too far from it, he might like to spend a few days touring this natural wonder, she suggested. They could talk more about her experiments when he returned.

When Levi accepted this idea, Levi-Montalcini sighed with relief. During the three days he was gone, she carefully drew the patterns of fibers she saw under the microscope, tracing their route from the sympathetic ganglia to the organs and veins of the embryo. Levi studied the drawings after his return and grumblingly admitted that she might just possibly be right, but he still insisted, "I don't believe it."

Levi-Montalcini knew she needed additional evidence to convince Levi and, perhaps, other scientists who might doubt her results when she published them. To obtain it, she decided to use a slightly different system. Instead of transplanting the tumor tissue onto embryos themselves, she would graft the tissue onto the protective membrane that grew around the embryos. The membrane was laced by blood vessels that grew into each embryo, carrying nutrients from the egg's yolk, but it contained no nerves. This system would let liquids from the tumor reach the embryos through the blood vessels, but any direct contact between the cancerous tissue and the embryos' nerve tissue would be prevented.

After performing each transplant, Levi-Montalcini made a small window in the egg's hard shell, through which she could peer with her stereomicroscope every day. (To protect the embryo from germs, she covered the hole with a piece of adhesive tape after each viewing.) She saw the same wild nerve growth that she had witnessed before, confirming her belief that the "nerve-growth promoting agent," as she had begun to call it, had to be a liquid coming from the tumor.

Levi-Montalcini described her results in a letter to Renato Dulbecco in early January 1951, and he wrote back with enthusiasm, calling her discovery "sensational." After doing additional work, she also presented her findings at a symposium sponsored by the New York Academy of Sciences a little later in the year. Paul Weiss, the eminent embryologist Levi-Montalcini had met earlier, termed her paper the most exciting discovery of the year. An attack of pain from a kidney ailment spoiled her moment of triumph, however. She had to hurry back to St. Louis and undergo emergency surgery for it.

Revelations in Rio

Now came the difficult, perhaps impossible, task of trying to find out what the growth-promoting agent was. Levi-Montalcini's attempts to reproduce the nerve growth by injecting extracts from the tumors into whole chick embryos failed, so she decided to use a different and simpler system. She might have better luck, she thought, if she grew embryo nerve tissue along with pieces of the tumor tissue in vitro—that is, in tissue culture. Tissue culture would also speed up her work, allowing her to see results in hours instead of weeks. She had learned how to grow embryonic nerve tissue in culture during her medical school studies with Giuseppe Levi, but her laboratory at Washington University was not equipped for this technique.

Fortunately, Levi-Montalcini knew someone who could give her just the help she needed: a German-Jewish scientist named Hertha Meyer, who had worked with Levi on some of his tissue culture projects in the mid-1930s. Meyer had come to Italy in 1933 to escape the Nazis, then moved to Brazil in 1939 when Italy, too, became dangerous for Jews, especially foreign-born ones. Meyer now headed a tissue culture laboratory at the Institute of Biophysics in Rio de Janeiro. Levi-Montalcini asked Meyer if she could come to Brazil and carry out her experiments in Meyer's laboratory. After consulting with the institute's director, Meyer assured Levi-Montalcini that she would be welcome, and Viktor Hamburger helped Levi-Montalcini arrange a grant from the Rockefeller Foundation to pay for her trip.

Levi-Montalcini flew to Brazil in September 1952. Tucked in a box inside her coat were two tiny stowaways: a pair of mice bearing the tumors she wanted to test. Hertha Meyer met Levi-Montalcini at the airport and took her to Copacabana, where she had arranged for the visiting scientist to stay with friends. Levi-Montalcini's room proved to be pleasant except for periodic invasions by giant tropical cockroaches, which fortunately her landlord's basset hound was happy to hunt down and devour. She rode from there to the laboratory each day in one of the city's crowded, open streetcars, usually clinging to the edge of the platform and praying she would not fall off.

The next four months were, Sharon McGrayne quotes Levi-Montalcini as saying, "one of the most intense periods of my life." During those months, as Levi-Montalcini performed her research in Meyer's laboratory, she sent a series of drawings and letters to Viktor Hamburger describing her successes and failures. Hamburger saved the letters and returned them to her many years later, when he heard that she was working on her autobiography. At the time of receiving

Tissue Culture: Keeping Cells Alive

Perhaps the first successful attempt at keeping animal organs or tissues alive outside the body came in the 1880s, when British physiologist Sydney Ringer (1835–1910) developed a salt solution in which an isolated frog heart could continue beating for a short period. Ross Harrison (1870–1959), a biologist in the United States, extended this work to tissues and cells in 1907, when he grew nerve tissue from a frog embryo in a drop of frog lymph (a fluid produced by the body's immune system). Harrison placed the lymph on a cover slip, a thin piece of glass used to cover a specimen on a microscope slide. After the lymph clotted (thickened), he turned the cover slip over and placed it on top of a microscope slide that contained a depression, or well, in the center. The drop of jellylike fluid then hung down into the well, suspended from the cover slip. This "hanging drop" technique had been used before to grow bacteria, but Harrison was the first to use it on tissue. Looking through a microscope, he was able to watch nerve fibers developing in the tissue over time.

Two researchers working at New York's Rockefeller Institute (later Rockefeller University), French-born Alexis Carrel (1873–1944) and Montrose Burrows, extended Harrison's techniques further. Using plasma (the liquid part of blood) from chickens as their solution rather than frog lymph, they adapted his hanging drop method to grow cells from birds and mammals. (Rita Levi-Montalcini used chicken plasma in her embryonic nerve tissue cultures as well.) In 1910, Carrel and Burrows announced that they had grown both normal and cancerous cells from chickens, rats, dogs, and humans in their laboratory.

(continues on page 69)

(Opposite page) *Ross Harrison invented the first successful technique for tissue culture in 1907. (1) Harrison put a drop of lymph, a clear fluid, from a frog onto a thin square of glass called a cover slip and placed a small amount of frog nerve tissue inside the drop. (2) After a while, the lymph clotted, or thickened. The drop would then stay in place when Harrison turned the cover slip upside down. He placed the inverted cover slip over a glass microscope slide with a depression, or well, in the center. (3) The tissue grew in the drop of lymph suspended over the well in the microscope slide. Harrison could place the slide under his microscope and watch the nerve cells multiply.*

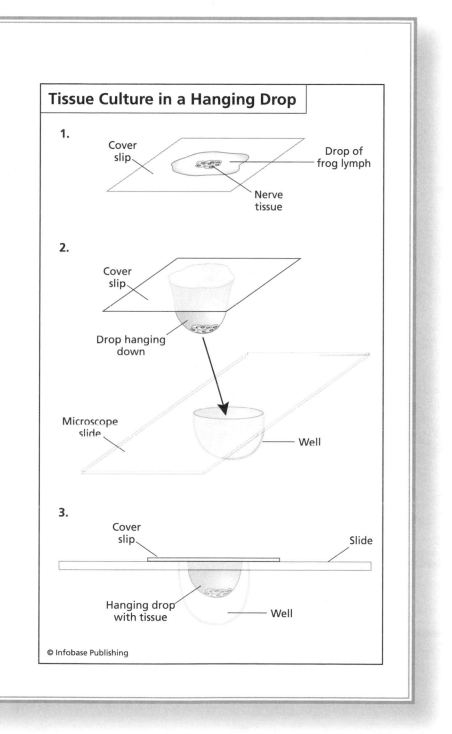

Tissue Culture in a Hanging Drop

1.

Cover slip

Drop of frog lymph

Nerve tissue

2.

Cover slip

Drop hanging down

Microscope slide

Well

3.

Cover slip

Slide

Hanging drop with tissue

Well

© Infobase Publishing

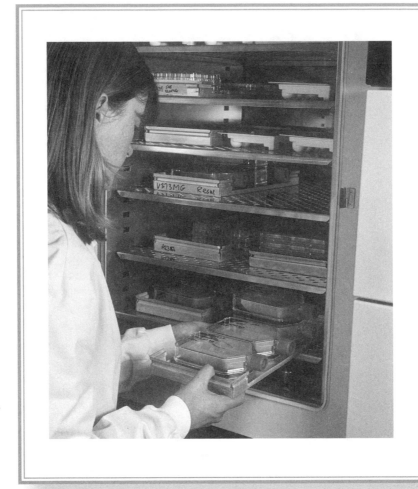

the letters, he wrote to her that they "show[ed] beautifully how real research works, ups and downs, despair and triumph."

At first, the work went badly. When placed next to sympathetic and sensory ganglia cut from eight-day-old chick embryos and grown in vitro, the mouse tumor tissues did not produce the nerve growth that they had done in whole embryos. They also stopped the growth of supporting cells that usually occurred when such ganglia were grown by themselves or with other parts of a normal embryo. Perhaps, Levi-Montalcini thought, in this new system the tumors

(continued from page 66)

Carrel and Burrows went on to add other materials, including chicken embryo extract, to their cultures. These improvements allowed the men to raise larger groups of cells and keep them alive for longer periods of time. Most strikingly, Carrel kept part of a chicken embryo's heart beating from 1912 to 1946. Every January 17, the anniversary of the culture's establishment, Carrel and some of his staff sang "Happy Birthday" to their chicken heart. The heart, in fact, outlived Carrel by two years.

Tissue culture allowed scientists to study the development of embryonic tissues, growth of normal tissues, and changes that occurred in cells that became cancerous. It paved the way for tissue and organ transplants and for tissue banks, which supply material for some types of transplants. Tissue culture is also essential for production of vaccines against virus-caused diseases such as polio, because the viruses used in these vaccines must be grown inside living cells. Today, "lines" of cells kept in cultures are used in research on stem cells, which may eventually lead to treatments for conditions including spinal cord injury and Alzheimer's disease.

(Opposite page) *Tissue culture is used today in many scientific laboratories. Researchers use culture to learn about normal and cancerous tissue growth, prepare vaccines, and study stem cells, which potentially can grow into any type of cell in the body and may someday be used as "miracle cure" medical treatments.* (Simon Fraser/MRC Unit, Newcastle General Hospital/Photo Researchers, Inc.)

were producing some harmful substance that masked the nerve growth effect.

Racking her brain for a way around this difficulty, Levi-Montalcini remembered noticing in St. Louis that the appearance of the mouse cancer cells changed after they had grown next to whole chick embryos. Also, she had sometimes transplanted the same piece of tumor tissue several times from one embryo to another, and she recalled that the tissue's power to stimulate nerve growth and differentiation had become stronger with each trans-

Rita Levi-Montalcini made some of her most exciting discoveries in Rio de Janeiro, Brazil, shown here with nearby Sugarloaf Mountain. She found the cultured cells under her microscope and the carnival atmosphere of the city equally thrilling. (luminouslens, 2008, used under license from Shutterstock, Inc.)

plantation. Both of these observations suggested that growth next to the embryos altered the cancer cells in some way that affected their action on embryonic nerves. If this was true, then tumor tissue that had already grown next to a chick embryo might stimulate the chick ganglia in culture, even though tissue taken directly from the mice had failed to do so.

That proved to be exactly what happened, turning Levi-Montalcini's despair into excitement. Within six to 10 hours, sensory and sympathetic ganglia grown next to previously transplanted tumors in tissue culture sprouted a thick halo of nerve fibers "like the rays of the sun," as she said in an *Omni* magazine interview. Lacking a camera, she drew pictures of the amazing halos with India ink, then sent them to Viktor Hamburger by express airmail. Even extracts from the embryos that had carried the tumors produced the stimulation effect, again suggesting that the growth factor was a liquid. Ganglia grown next to other mouse tumors or to normal embryonic mouse or chicken tissues showed no halo effect, however.

Repeating these experiments during November and growing the two tissues together for longer periods of time (several days instead of only one), Levi-Montalcini obtained even clearer results. The side of the ganglia that was next to the tumor tissue showed much more intense nerve fiber growth than the side farther away, and the fibers seemed to be growing primarily toward the tumor. This suggested, as some of her earlier observations had also done, that the mystery substance attracted nerve fibers toward itself as well as stimulating their growth.

A Masked Figure Appears

A puzzling question remained, however. Although the actions of the tumor tissue on whole embryos and on ganglia in culture both involved nerve growth, the appearance of the two effects was so different that Levi-Montalcini could not be sure that the same substance caused them both. She thought of two ways of checking this: by seeing whether types of tumor that did not produce nerve growth in whole embryos produced it in her culture system, and by seeing what effect noncancerous mouse tissue had.

Results from the first method of checking supported Levi-Montalcini's belief that the same substance caused both nerve growth effects. Tumors that did not stimulate nerve growth in whole embryos did not stimulate growth in cultured ganglia, either. The outcome of her tests of normal mouse tissue, however, was as startling as it was dismaying. Although the effect of normal mouse tissue was not as strong as that of the sarcoma tissue, the normal tissue also made nerve fibers grow while blocking the growth and spread of supporting cells, just as the tumor cells did. This suggested that the effect was simply caused somehow by mouse tissue in general and was stronger in the tumor tissue only because the cancer cells multiplied faster. Levi-Montalcini wrote to Hamburger that this result was "the most severe blow to my enthusiasm that I could ever have suffered."

In the classic version of the scientific method, scientists let the results of their experiments guide their thinking. They begin by asking a question and forming an educated guess, or hypothesis, about what the answer might be. In this case, Levi-Montalcini had asked how the mouse tumors had made the nerve cells grow. She had hypothesized that the tumor cells gave off some chemical that caused this effect. She had also hypothesized that only tumor cells contained the growth-inducing substance, a logical guess since cancers are known for their abnormally rapid growth.

After forming a hypothesis, scientists carry out experiments to test their idea. If repeated experiments suggest that a hypothesis is wrong, the researchers are supposed to change the hypothesis and try again. Levi-Montalcini, however, broke this rule. Her instinct said that the nerve growth effect of the normal mouse tissue and that of the tumor tissue were different in some fundamental way, and she refused to abandon this idea. Instead, she decided to ignore the puzzling effect of the normal mouse tissues for the time being and continue to concentrate on the tumor tissues. Perhaps, she thought, she could return to the "mouse effect" later and find an explanation for it.

With her mind at ease once more, Levi-Montalcini spent her last month in Rio playing tourist, a luxury she had not allowed herself before. The month was January, just before the annual festival of Carnaval. Levi-Montalcini loved watching the excited preparations as people decorated their costumes and practiced their singing and drumming. She was not able to stay for Carnaval itself, but she attended a pre-Carnaval ceremony in which the Brazilians brought candles, flowers, and offerings to the shore to honor Iemanjá, the goddess of the ocean. She was thrilled to see this ritual, in which wealthy citizens and poor people from the city's slums, or favelas, took part side by side. A variety of races was also represented—white, black, Indian, and mixtures of all three. Coming from a country where class distinctions and, at least briefly, racial ones had been so rigid, she found the sight immensely moving. She wrote later, "I, too, lit a candle in my mind in honor of that marvelous crucible of different races."

Even though Levi-Montalcini never saw Brazil's Carnaval, that festival affected her thinking about the scientific discovery she was in the process of making. In her mind, the growth factor she was struggling to identify began to take on a life of its own as a mysterious masked figure, much like those beginning to crowd Rio's streets.

"The tumor factor had given a first hint of its existence in St. Louis," she wrote in *Saga of the Nerve Growth Factor,* "but it was in Rio de Janeiro that it revealed itself . . . in a theatrical and grandiose way, as if spurred by the bright atmosphere of that explosive and exuberant manifestation of life that is the carnival in Rio."

"Together We
Are Wonderful"

Convinced that her discovery in Rio would provide the "philosopher's stone" for understanding the nature of the nerve growth–promoting factor, Rita Levi-Montalcini celebrated by taking a brief tour of Peru and Ecuador before returning home. She wandered through the ancient Inca ruins of Machu Picchu and saw the Incas' descendants selling their wares in the marketplaces of mountain towns. Excited as she was about her work, she found it refreshing to escape the laboratory for a little while.

When Levi-Montalcini returned to St. Louis in late January 1953, she learned of another reason to celebrate. Waiting for her at the airport with Viktor Hamburger was a new coworker, Stanley Cohen. Hamburger had written to Levi-Montalcini while she was still in Rio that he was hiring Cohen to join her project as a research associate. Cohen was a biochemist, and his task

Stanley Cohen (1922–   ):
Discoverer of Growth Factors

Stanley Cohen was born in Brooklyn, New York, on November 17, 1922, to a Russian Jewish immigrant tailor and his wife. He earned his bachelor's degree from Brooklyn College, which offered free tuition for city residents, with a double major in biology and chemistry in 1943. Even in his undergraduate days, he was drawn to the study of cells and to what, in his Nobel Prize autobiographical sketch, he calls "the mysteries of embryonic development." He wanted to use chemistry to understand these biological puzzles.

Cohen worked for a while as a bacteriologist in a dairy to earn enough money to pay for graduate school. He obtained a master's degree in zoology from Oberlin College in Ohio in 1945, then a Ph.D. in biochemistry from the University of Michigan, Ann Arbor, in 1948. For his Ph.D. project, on the way the bodies of earthworms used certain chemicals, he spent many nights digging up thousands of worms from the moist soil of the university campus. Cohen wrote in his Nobel sketch that he believed his "ability to stomach-tube earthworms," in turn, led to his postdoctoral assignment in the pediatrics and biochemistry departments of the University of Colorado, where he studied the metabolism of premature babies. He first came to Washington University in 1952 to learn how to use radioactive materials in biological research.

Cohen worked with Rita Levi-Montalcini on nerve growth factor from 1953 to 1959, research that would lead to a shared Nobel Prize in physiology or medicine in 1986 (as well as other shared awards, including the Lasker Award for Basic Medical Research, which the two also won in 1986). After leaving Washington University because he was unable to obtain a tenured position there, Cohen moved to Vanderbilt University, in Nashville, Tennessee, initially as an assistant professor of biochemistry. He became an American Cancer Society Research Professor at the university in 1976 and a distinguished professor in 1986. He retired in 2000.

Cohen's many honors were awarded, not only because of his work with Levi-Montalcini, but also because of his discovery of a second growth factor, epidermal growth factor (EGF). His research on this factor began while he was still at Washington University, when he noticed that newborn mice treated with an unpurified

(continues on next page)

(continued from previous page)

extract of NGF from mouse salivary glands opened their eyes much sooner than normal. (Mice, like puppies and kittens, are born with their eyes shut and normally open them about two weeks after birth.) Their teeth also grew in sooner than those of normal baby mice. Purified NGF did not produce these effects, however.

The unpurified extract proved to contain a second growth factor, which Cohen isolated in 1962. He named the substance epidermal growth factor in 1965 because he had found that the substance produced the changes in the baby mice by making the outer layer of skin, or epidermis, grow faster than normal. He worked out the factor's structure and amino acid sequence, which he described in papers published in 1972. "You just keep on trying to find things," he said after winning the Nobel Prize.

Stanley Cohen, a biochemist, worked with Rita Levi-Montalcini at Washington University from 1953 to 1959. He determined the chemical identity of nerve growth factor, the growth-promoting substance she had discovered, and found several new sources for it. Later, at Vanderbilt University in Tennessee, he discovered a second growth factor, epidermal growth factor. Cohen shared the Nobel Prize in physiology or medicine with Levi-Montalcini in 1986. (The Washington University in St. Louis Magazine)

would be to work out the chemical nature of the substance that Levi-Montalcini had discovered.

Lucky Snakebite

Stanley Cohen, limping a little because of a childhood bout with polio and usually accompanied by his dog Smog, "the sweetest and most mongrel dog I ever saw" as Rita Levi-Montalcini put it, became a familiar sight in Levi-Montalcini's laboratory. She paid equally frequent visits to Cohen's lab, two floors below. As had been the case with Levi-Montalcini and Viktor Hamburger, she and Cohen found that they had much to learn from each other: Levi-Montalcini knew almost nothing about biochemistry, and Cohen was equally uninformed about the nervous system.

From the beginning, Cohen and Levi-Montalcini realized that their skills complemented each other perfectly. So did their approaches to scientific work: Levi-Montalcini admired Cohen's steady, one-step-at-a-time attitude, and he, in turn, respected her intuitive leaps. As Cohen exclaimed one day, "Rita, you and I are good, but together we are wonderful." Viktor Hamburger also dropped in on many of their conferences, although he did not carry out research on their project.

Levi-Montalcini began by setting up in her laboratory a tissue culture system similar to the one she had used in Rio. Her first task was to confirm the results she had seen in Brazil, which she succeeded in doing. She also had to help Cohen in the formidable task of trying to identify what he and Levi-Montalcini eventually decided to call nerve growth factor (NGF). To provide a single sample large enough for Cohen to test, she had to extract the factor from dozens of tumor nodules grown on embryos.

After a year of hard work for both partners, Cohen concluded in 1954 that the mystery factor, still only partly purified, appeared to be a nucleoprotein—a combination of nucleic acid and protein. He thought, however, that the nucleic acid might not really be an essential part of the factor. To find out whether that was true, he needed a way to remove the nucleic acid from the mixture; Levi-Montalcini could then use her tissue culture system to determine whether the remaining material still produced the growth effect.

When Cohen mentioned his problem to Arthur Kornberg, a fellow biochemist (and fellow future Nobel Prize winner) then working at Washington University, Kornberg told him that venom from the water moccasin, a poisonous snake, contained an enzyme that broke down nucleic acids. Cohen therefore obtained some venom (which was used in treatments for snakebite) and mixed a small amount of the factor with it.

Cohen gave the venom-treated sample to Levi-Montalcini to test, along with several other samples modified in other ways or left alone, one spring day in 1956. As is commonly done in science experiments, he did not tell her which sample was which, so that she would not be tempted to see what she expected or hoped to see when she examined her nerve tissue. (In tests on humans to determine the effectiveness of new drugs, for instance, neither the patients being tested nor the doctors evaluating the results know until the end of the test whether particular patients were given the new drug or instead received a placebo, a harmless substance that should have no effect on a patient's medical condition.)

To Levi-Montalcini's amazement, one of the samples in that batch produced far more nerve growth than any of the others—what she later called "a stupendous halo." Sure enough, when Cohen consulted his notes, he found that it was the one he had treated with the water moccasin venom. When he saw the effect for himself under the microscope, Cohen said, "Rita, I am afraid that with this we have used up all our good luck."

Cohen and Levi-Montalcini realized that either of two things could have produced the result they saw. First, the venom might have destroyed some inhibiting material that remained in the impure sample, making the factor's growth effect stronger than ever. Alternatively, the venom itself could have contained the nerve growth factor or something very similar. Choosing between these explanations was easy: They simply added a little purified moccasin venom to one of Levi-Montalcini's nerve tissue cultures. The venom produced a tremendous amount of nerve growth.

Levi-Montalcini and Cohen realized that this discovery had several exciting implications. First, it gave them a source of NGF that yielded far more of the material than the tiny tumor nodules

By a lucky accident, Stanley Cohen discovered that the venom of the water moccasin or cottonmouth, shown here, was a rich source of nerve growth factor. (Rusty Dodson, 2008, used under license from Shutterstock, Inc.)

had provided. (When Cohen purified the part of the venom that produced nerve growth, he found that it was 1,000 times richer in NGF than the tumor tissue.) Second, it meant that NGF had to be a protein, since nucleic acid could not survive in the venom.

Between 1956 and 1958, Cohen continued trying to pin down the chemical nature of the factor. He found it to be a protein with a molecular weight of 20,000. (Molecular weight is the sum of the weights of all the atoms in a molecule.) Levi-Montalcini, meanwhile, tested the factor's effects on whole living things. She found that when the substance obtained from the venom was injected into four-to-eight-day-old chick embryos, it produced the same nerve growth effect as the mouse tumor tissue, just as it did in the tissue culture. This confirmed that the factor was not produced only by cancer cells and that its "magic" was not limited to cultured specimens. In a 1958 paper, Levi-Montalcini described these results and gave what she called "irrefutable evidence" that the effects on whole embryos and on cultured nerve tissue, though very different in some respects, were produced by the same substance.

Proteins: Workhorses of the Cell

Proteins are a large class of biomolecules that do most of the work in cells. Their name, given by Swedish chemist Jöns Jakob Berzelius in 1838, comes from a Greek word meaning "first" or "most important."

Protein Synthesis

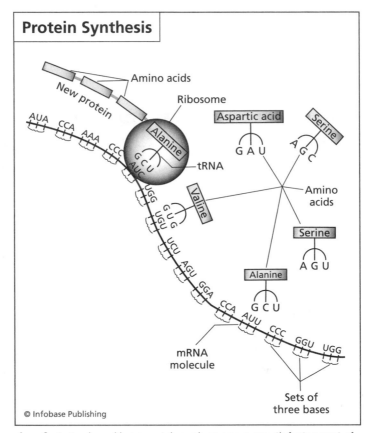

© Infobase Publishing

As a first step in making a protein such as nerve growth factor, part of a DNA molecule (a gene) uses itself as a pattern to form a matching stretch of messenger RNA (mRNA). When the messenger RNA moves into the cytoplasm of the cell, it attracts matching short stretches of transfer RNA (tRNA), each of which tows a single amino acid molecule. With the help of an organelle called a ribosome, the transfer RNA molecules lock onto the matching parts of the messenger RNA, and the amino acids they carry are joined, forming a protein.

Proteins consist of long chains of smaller molecules called amino acids, assembled in a particular order and coiled into complex three-dimensional shapes. Twenty types of amino acids are known in the natural world. Small proteins, sometimes termed peptides, may be made up of only a few dozen of these molecules, while the largest protein known, a muscle protein called titin, contains almost 27,000. An average protein is composed of several hundred amino acids. Each kind of protein has a unique sequence of amino acids and a unique shape.

The recipes for making proteins are contained in the cell's genetic material—its DNA. Like protein molecules, molecules of DNA and its sister nucleic acid, RNA (ribonucleic acid), are made up of smaller molecules. The small molecules within nucleic acids, called bases, are strung together along a "backbone" of sugar and phosphate molecules. There are four types of bases. Francis Crick and other scientists discovered in the 1960s that the order, or sequence, of bases in DNA determines the sequence of amino acids in the proteins that the cell makes. Each group of three bases is a "letter" in what has come to be called the genetic code. The 64 (4 x 4 x 4) possible combinations of three bases provide more than enough letters to stand for the 20 amino acids that can make up a protein.

When a gene carrying the code for a particular type of protein turns on, that stretch of DNA makes a copy of itself in the form of RNA. Unlike DNA, this RNA, termed messenger RNA, can pass from the nucleus into the main body of the cell. There, organelles called ribosomes collect amino acids and link them together in the order specified by the RNA.

Enzymes are perhaps the most important group of proteins. These substances greatly speed up chemical reactions within the cell; indeed, without enzymes, the reactions essentially would not happen. The enzymes begin the reactions by attaching, or binding, to other proteins or other substances that will be involved in the reactions. The approximately 4,000 reactions aided by enzymes allow cells to store and use energy, repair themselves, reproduce, and much more. The enzymes themselves are not changed by the reactions.

Every task that cells perform depends on proteins to some extent. Cells and organisms are able to move because of proteins that can stretch and contract, for instance. Other proteins give cells

(continues on next page)

(continued from previous page)

their shape and allow the cells to maintain it. Proteins carry materials in body fluids; the protein hemoglobin, for example, carries oxygen in the blood and gives the blood its red color. Proteins such as nerve growth factor convey signals from one cell to another, often activating enzymes or other proteins in a complex chain of events that results in such major changes as cell growth, reproduction, or death. Some proteins turn genes on or off. According to John W. Kimball, a retired Harvard professor and biology textbook author, "proteins are truly the physical basis of life."

A New Source of Nerve Growth Factor

If the same substance could be extracted from sources as different as snake venom and mouse cancer tissue, Levi-Montalcini and Cohen realized that it most likely existed in other animal tissues as well. But which ones? Levi-Montalcini's tissue culture system could help the two answer this question in a reasonable length of time because it let them screen hundreds of samples for NGF activity in just a few hours. Still, testing a wide variety of tissues could have taken months, if not years.

Fortunately, Cohen remembered an odd fact about mice that provided the pair with a shortcut. Just as humans do, mice produce saliva from glands in their mouths. This liquid begins the process of breaking down and digesting food. In mice, though, some of the salivary glands are much bigger in males than in females. In addition to saliva, these glands make a mild poison that the mice inject when they bite. (Females produce a little of this toxin too, but males make much more.) Male mice, like males of many other animal species, fight over females, biting and clawing each other, and the poison produced by their salivary glands helps the mice weaken their opponents.

Even though the mouse toxin is not strong enough to kill, Cohen realized that in many ways the compound was comparable to snake venom. For instance, the glands in the reptile's mouth that make its venom also make substances that aid in digestion; these glands, in fact, are the equivalent of a mammal's salivary glands. Cohen therefore suggested to Levi-Montalcini in 1958 that they begin their search for other sources of NGF by testing extracts from male mouse salivary glands.

This proved to be a lucky hunch. Even when diluted to the equivalent of the extract of one gland in 13.2 gallons (50 l) of solution, the mouse gland extracts produced nerve growth greater than any Levi-Montalcini and Cohen had seen before.

Levi-Montalcini and Cohen went on to test one mouse tissue after another in an attempt to find out what else might contain the mystery molecule. They discovered that all the tissues stimulated some degree of nerve growth, though not nearly as much as the salivary gland extract had done. Levi-Montalcini realized that this finding explained the disturbing "mouse effect" that she had encountered in Rio. In fact, she and other researchers eventually learned that cells from a wide variety of tissues and species of vertebrate animals produce measurable quantities of NGF.

Effects on Living Animals

Now using mouse salivary glands as their source of NGF, Levi-Montalcini and Cohen set to work with a new will. They performed their most intense experiments between winter 1958 and summer 1959. Cohen concentrated on purifying the mouse version of the factor and finding out the chemical details of its nature, such as its molecular weight. He confirmed that the growth-promoting compound from snake venom and the one from mouse glands had essentially identical chemical features. The molecular weight of the mouse protein was twice that of the snake one, however. Cohen concluded that in the mouse the factor existed in the form of two units of protein combined into a single molecule, while in the water moccasin the protein units occurred separately.

While Cohen was carrying out this work, Levi-Montalcini tested the factor's effects on mice and rats of various ages. She found that injections of the substance, given daily for three weeks, made the sympathetic ganglia in newborn mice and rats grow 10 times larger than they normally would have. The quantity of nerve fibers growing into the animals' organs and tissues increased as well. Similar injections also increased nerve growth in adult animals, but not as strikingly. Levi-Montalcini and Cohen published papers about their discoveries during this period, but Levi-Montalcini said in her Nobel Prize lecture that they "did not at first find enthusiastic reception by the scientific community . . . [because the discoveries] did not fit into any conceptual preexisting schemes, nor did [they] seem to bear any relation to normal control mechanisms at work during ontogenesis [development]."

In 1959, Levi-Montalcini and Cohen decided to, in essence, run their experiments in reverse—in other words, to find out what happened to the developing nervous system if the action of nerve growth factor was completely blocked. As part of its job of protecting the body against bacteria and other invaders, the immune system produces substances called antibodies, which destroy foreign material to which the system has been exposed. Each type of antibody reacts to only one kind of substance. Antiserums, or liquids containing antibodies against particular substances, can be created by exposing immune cells to those substances. Antiserums to snake venom already existed—they are used to treat snakebite—and Levi-Montalcini found that snake venom antiserum blocked the formation of nerve fiber halos in her tissue culture system. She and Cohen therefore decided to create an antiserum to the NGF from mouse glands and see what effect it would have.

Levi-Montalcini found that antiserum to mouse NGF stopped nerve growth in vitro, just as the snake antiserum did. She then went on to test the antiserum on living animals. The results were just as startling as the nerve growth she and Cohen had seen earlier. After a month of daily injections, the sympathetic ganglia along the spinal cords of newborn mice and rats were almost completely destroyed. The rest of the mice's nervous systems developed normally, however, and, amazingly, the overall health of the animals seemed to be unaffected. (Other researchers later used this "immunosympathectomy" technique in experiments aimed at learning more about the sympathetic nervous system in health and disease.)

Viktor Hamburger, who stopped by Levi-Montalcini's laboratory on the day that she made this discovery, said she should make a note of the date—June 11, 1959—because it marked "a memorable event in neuroembryology." Her finding showed that NGF was not merely something that could produce an odd stimulation of nerve growth. Rather, certain types of nerves apparently depended completely on this substance in order to develop properly or even stay alive. Levi-Montalcini and Cohen published two articles on their work in the *Proceedings of the National Academy of Sciences* in 1960.

Unfortunately, this time of exciting codiscovery, which Levi-Montalcini in her autobiography called "the six most intense and productive years of my life," came to an end shortly after her mouse experiments. At the end of 1958, Hamburger had sadly told Cohen and Levi-Montalcini that his department could not afford to offer Cohen a permanent research position. Levi-Montalcini heard the news, she wrote, "like the tolling of a funeral bell." Cohen, with his own family to think of, decided that he needed to seek a better-paid position elsewhere. He found it at Vanderbilt University, in Tennessee, and he and Levi-Montalcini parted in July 1959. A new arrival, an Italian biochemist named Pietro Angeletti (or Piero, as Levi-Montalcini called him), took over Cohen's position on Levi-Montalcini's team.

Return to Rome

During all the years Rita Levi-Montalcini lived in the United States, she had exchanged frequent letters with her family in Italy, especially her mother and her twin, Paola. She had followed the growth of Paola's increasingly successful career as an artist, for instance, although Paola tended to be far less forthcoming in her letters than was Rita. Levi-Montalcini had made monthlong visits to the family each summer as well.

Around 1961, however, Levi-Montalcini found herself missing her mother and sisters and brother more and more. For one thing, she knew that her mother was growing older, and the two might not have many more years to enjoy together. She decided, therefore, that she would like to live in Italy for part of each year.

Going Home

Although Levi-Montalcini had become a U.S. citizen in 1956, she had kept her Italian citizenship as well, so having a residence in both countries would present no legal problems. However, she did not want her return to Italy to end her research on nerve growth factor or her connection with Washington University, where she had been a full professor since 1958. She had met a number of Italian scientists who were interested in studying NGF during a conference on the factor in 1960, so she developed the idea of establishing a small research unit in Italy that would collaborate with the university. She presented her idea to Viktor Hamburger, and Hamburger, in turn, spoke to the medical school's dean. The dean gave permission for Levi-Montalcini to spend several months of each year in Rome to establish and work with the unit, while Pietro Angeletti directed her laboratory in the United States. She also won a grant for the project from the National Science Foundation, a U.S. federal government funding agency, and left for Rome in spring 1961.

The Italian government of the day was not known for its support of science, according to Levi-Montalcini, but it welcomed her small unit. She obtained laboratory space and equipment from the country's Institute of Health (Istituto Superiore di Sanità) and a little additional funding from its National Research Council (Consiglio Nazionale delle Richerche, or CNR). Her research quarters in Rome were soon larger than those she had at Washington University. She had no trouble recruiting young scientists for her new team, even though she could offer only a minimal salary. Italian postdoctoral students were eager to work with someone of her reputation, and many hoped to gain a chance to continue their research in the United States as well.

Coordinating the work of groups so far apart geographically was difficult at first, but Levi-Montalcini and Pietro Angeletti, who also had family members in Italy and wanted to spend more time there, worked out a solution to this problem: They would alternate as heads of the two groups. That way, each could spend part of the year in St. Louis and part in Rome.

Readjusting to life and work in Italy also presented some challenges for Levi-Montalcini. As she had planned, she saw more of her family and Italian friends than had been possible before, but by the same token, she had less time to spend with equally valued friends and colleagues in the Midwest. In addition, she had become accustomed to the relaxed attitude of the students on the Washington University campus and found it strange to be treated with the formality that European students still accorded to their professors.

During the months she was in Italy, Levi-Montalcini traveled to Turin every weekend to visit her mother, who was now quite elderly and ill with asthma. Levi-Montalcini was in the United States, however, when she learned in June 1963 that Adele Levi had fallen, breaking her thighbone. Surgeons inserted a metal pin in Mrs. Levi's leg to help the bones rejoin, but she was still in a wheelchair when Levi-Montalcini visited her in July. Her condition improved enough for her, in turn, to visit Rita and Paola in Rome in September. The whole family was with Mrs. Levi in Turin later that month when she had a second surgery to remove the pin in her leg. She seemed to improve enough after the operation that Levi-Montalcini felt safe in returning to Rome for a few days to help a new researcher establish herself in the laboratory. Unfortunately, Mrs. Levi developed a fever and died before Levi-Montalcini could return. A weeping Paola broke the news to her by telephone.

Her mother was not Levi-Montalcini's only loss in the early 1960s. In late January 1965, she paid her last visit to her old mentor, Giuseppe Levi, in Turin's San Giovanni Hospital. Levi, by then 92 years old, had just been found to have terminal stomach cancer. He wasted no time on self-pity; instead, he asked Levi-Montalcini to tell him about her current work. At the end of their talk, according to Levi-Montalcini, he told her, "This is our last farewell. I thank you, Rita, for what you have done and hope your good fortune continues." Just as he had predicted during that visit, he died two weeks later.

Discoveries and Disappointments

During the portion of each year that Levi-Montalcini spent in Rome, she shared an apartment with Paola (who, like Levi-Montalcini herself, had never married) after their mother's death. There she watched the birth of Paola's works of art, which included engravings and large metal sculptures as well as paintings. (Critics said that Paola's art, fittingly for the sister of an architect, itself had an architectural feeling.) Speaking to Magdolna Hargittai in 2000, Levi-Montalcini, admittedly perhaps with some sisterly prejudice, said that Paola was "recognized as the best Italian woman artist of the century." The two made yearly trips together to visit art galleries and museums in Europe and the United States.

Living once more in Europe seemed to bring out the elegant and theatrical sides of Levi-Montalcini's personality. She restyled her hair from a bun to what Sharon McGrayne describes as "a dramatic swoop" and began wearing sleeveless, high-necked dresses with matching silk or brocade jackets, made especially for her. These stylish outfits became almost a uniform; she even wore them in the laboratory, with a standard protective coat over them. This way of dressing may have been one reason why Robert R. Provine, one of her former students, called her "Queen of Italy in a lab coat" in a 2003 article in the *St. Louis Post-Dispatch.* Echoing Provine, Levi-Montalcini's old friend Salvador Luria wrote in his autobiography, *A Slot*

Rita Levi-Montalcini showed her elegant side in her later life, when she divided her time between Italy and the United States. (Becker Medical Library, Washington University School of Medicine)

Genetic Engineering: Slicing and Dicing Genes

In 1973, scientists gained a new power that would have profound effects on Rita Levi-Montalcini's research—and on science and society as a whole: the ability to recombine and, eventually, alter

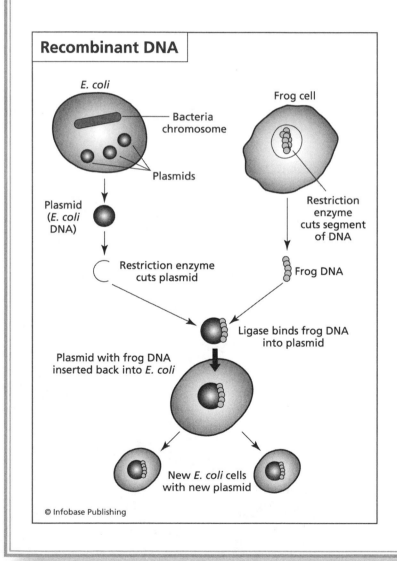

Recombinant DNA

© Infobase Publishing

genes at will. This ability, referred to originally as recombinant DNA, came to be known later as genetic engineering.

Genetic engineering grew out of the experiments of two California scientists, Stanley N. Cohen (no relation to the Stanley Cohen who worked with Levi-Montalcini) and Herbert Boyer. Using the bacterial restriction enzymes that Salvador Luria had discovered earlier, Boyer and Cohen cut apart plasmids, short, ring-shaped pieces of DNA found in bacteria. They combined plasmids from two types of bacteria into a single large plasmid, then transferred this plasmid into a third kind of bacteria. Each of the original plasmids carried a gene that conveyed resistance to a particular kind of antibiotic. The bacteria that received the combined plasmids had been susceptible to both kinds of antibiotics. After the transplant, however, these bacteria could grow in a culture dish containing both drugs. This proved that the two genes were still active in their new home.

As genetic engineering advanced in the late 1970s and 1980s, scientists became able to use bacteria as "factories" to copy, or clone, particular genes. Once researchers identified an interesting gene, they could cut the gene out of its original genome and transplant it into the genomes of bacteria. Bacteria reproduce quickly, doubling their number every 20 minutes or so—and each new copy of an engineered bacterium would contain the inserted gene. The gene could force the bacteria to make the protein for which it

(continues on next page)

(Opposite page) *In one of their groundbreaking gene-splicing experiments, Stanley Cohen and Herbert Boyer broke up cells of a common bacterium, E. coli, and took out small, ring-shaped pieces of DNA called plasmids. They then used a restriction enzyme to cut the plasmids open. They used the same enzyme to produce segments of DNA from the cells of frogs. The bacterial and frog DNA segments joined together because of the complementary "sticky ends" of single-stranded DNA attached to each segment. Boyer and Cohen used a ligase, another type of enzyme, to bind the segments together, creating a new plasmid that contained frog as well as bacterial DNA. The researchers then inserted the plasmids carrying the foreign genes into other E. coli bacteria and showed that the foreign genes could make their normal proteins. When the bacteria multiplied, the added genes were duplicated along with the bacteria's own genetic material.*

(continued from previous page)

carried the code, even if the bacteria would never make that protein in nature.

Biotechnology companies used gene cloning to manufacture unique biological products for use as drugs. The first of these drugs was genetically engineered human insulin, a substance that people with the disease diabetes need to take. Genentech, a company founded by Herbert Boyer and a business partner in 1976, began selling its recombinant insulin in 1982.

Scientists, meanwhile, cloned genes in order to make the genes' products available for study. Producing biological materials in this way was much more efficient than extracting them from such sources as animal tissues. The products were also pure, which the extracted versions often were not. Human and mouse genes carrying the code for nerve growth factor were identified in 1983, and Levi-Montalcini and other scientists began working with pure NGF produced by genetic engineering a year later.

Machine, A Broken Test Tube, that Levi-Montalcini received "the nickname 'the queen' because of her impeccable dresses and regal manner." Sharon McGrayne mentions that during this period, Levi-Montalcini liked to entertain friends and visiting scientists and became famous for her dinner parties.

During the 1960s, Levi-Montalcini's two research groups made progress on learning how NGF acts in cells. For example, their electron microscope studies revealed that a major effect of NGF was to stimulate production of neurofilaments and neurotubules, which play an important role in transporting substances within nerve cells. (Levi-Montalcini also had a chance to work briefly with Stanley Cohen once more around 1964 when, during a sabbatical he spent at her unit in Rome, she helped him carry out tissue-culture studies of epidermal growth factor, the new factor he had discovered several years before.) Levi-Montalcini claimed in her autobiography that at this time, in spite of some interest that had been stirred by the articles that she and Stanley Cohen had written about the factor in the mid-1950s, her laboratories were almost the only groups system-atically studying nerve growth factor.

The small research unit that Levi-Montalcini had founded, called the Center of Neurobiology, was taken over by the CNR and became part of a new Laboratory for Cell Biology in 1969. In addi-tion to Levi-Montalcini's neurobiology department, that institution had departments devoted to cell biology, immunology (the study of the immune system), and mechanisms of gene expression. Levi-Montalcini was made director of the entire laboratory. According to Sharon McGrayne, she had originally planned to share the direc-torship with Pietro Angeletti, who had helped to arrange funding for the institute, but Angeletti took a better-paying position with a drug company instead. "Their friendship did not survive the blow," McGrayne wrote.

Disappointment over Angeletti's departure was not the only reason why Levi-Montalcini had mixed feelings about her unit's expansion. She was unhappy that the new laboratory was in a crowded, traffic-packed area of downtown Rome. It also lacked the security force that had been available at Washington University, so working there at night did not seem safe to her. In addition, she felt that the CNR, swept up in the era's excitement about molecular biology and genetic engineering, no longer was really paying much attention to her research.

Levi-Montalcini had other causes for dissatisfaction during this period as well. Scientists' interest in NGF had increased in the late 1960s, after Stanley Cohen described epidermal growth fac-tor and other researchers began looking for additional members of what seemed likely to prove to be a large group of biologically critical compounds. As more articles on growth factors began to appear, however, Levi-Montalcini became discouraged about her own research because, as she complained in a 1988 interview for *Omni* magazine, "For a long time people didn't mention how NGF was discovered. My name was entirely left out of the literature. . . . I am not a person to be bitter, but it was astonishing to find it completely cancelled."

According to Sharon McGrayne's *Nobel Prize Women in Science,* some of Levi-Montalcini's colleagues felt that her perception of being rejected was exaggerated. Certainly she did not go without recognition during this period. In 1968, for instance, she was elected to the prestigious U.S. National Academy of Sciences—an honor given to only nine other women before her.

Ralph Bradshaw, who had been a member of Levi-Montalcini's Washington University team (he later moved to the University of California at Irvine), told Sharon McGrayne, "Rita was extremely possessive of NGF. She viewed it as her private property. It became her child. . . . There's almost no one in NGF [research] at one time or another who hasn't been at odds with her." Other former students and colleagues have also commented on Levi-Montalcini's tendency to drama. McGrayne wrote that Levi-Montalcini "move[d] mountains to help people in need," but those who knew the Italian scientist said that, like her mentor Giuseppe Levi, she did not tolerate stupidity well—or quietly. Some referred to the "Levi-Montalcini Roller Coaster" of emotions, and Robert Provine told a *St. Louis Post-Dispatch* reporter that working for her was like working for a combination of Marie Curie and dramatic Italian opera star Maria Callas.

Similarly, Levi-Montalcini wrote in her autobiography that lack of government support, coupled with a desire for independence, made many of her team members seek work elsewhere during this period, but others had different perceptions of the situation in her laboratory. Sharon McGrayne wrote that many scientists in the neurobiology unit in fact remained, even going for months without pay, because of their loyalty to Levi-Montalcini. On the other hand, in a biographical article in the winter 2000 issue of *Judaism*, Ruby Rohrlich stated that some workers left Levi-Montalcini's laboratory because they found her too "controlling [and] pressuring."

In any case, Levi-Montalcini felt so strongly about her perceived rejection by the scientific community that she gave up research on NGF for a few years, turning instead to studies of the nervous system of cockroaches. "*If they want NGF,* I thought, *they can have it,*" she said in the *Omni* interview. She claimed in that interview that her work on cockroaches "very successfully demonstrated how the nerve cells of insects interact with each other" and "developed an entirely new field of research in neuroscience."

Nonetheless, after a few years she decided that she could not give up NGF, which she, too, referred to as her "child." In 1972 she tried to dispose of the cockroaches—unsuccessfully, it appears, since she reported in the 1988 interview that some could still be seen in corners of her laboratory at night—and went back to her true life's work.

Links to Many Systems

Meanwhile, work on NGF proceeded, in Levi-Montalcini's laboratories and others. In the 1960s, Pietro Angeletti and a member of Levi-Montalcini's Italian team, chemist Vincenzo Bocchini, had greatly improved the technique for purifying NGF from mouse salivary glands. Two researchers on the Washington University team, Ralph Bradshaw and Ruth Hogue Angeletti, used their method to obtain pure samples of the compound and worked out the sequence of the amino acids that made up the NGF protein in 1971. They found that it was a relatively small molecule consisting of two identical chains, each 118 amino acids long.

Researchers were also finding out more about the way NGF interacts with other molecules in cells. They had learned that, like better-known signaling molecules called hormones, NGF and its cousin, Stanley Cohen's epidermal growth factor (EGF), begin their activity by attaching themselves to molecules termed receptors. These receptor molecules are set into the membranes of cells, with one part opening onto the surface of the cell and the other ending inside the cell. Each signaling molecule has its own type or types of receptor (some molecules can attach to several types), and the two fit together as a key fits into a lock. Only types of cells that have receptors for NGF can be affected by this factor.

The receptor for EGF had been identified in the late 1960s, and the receptor for NGF was found in the early 1970s. (In 1992, researchers learned that NGF can actually attach, or bind, to two different kinds of receptors.) In the mid-1970s, Stanley Cohen and other scientists found that when growth factor molecules attached to the outside of their receptors, the paired molecules, entwined like a loving couple, are carried inside the cell. Part of the receptor

Binding to Receptors

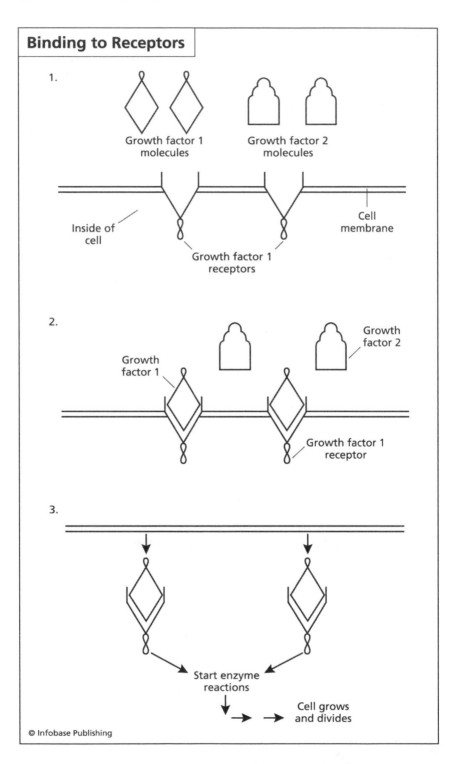

1.

Growth factor 1
molecules

Growth factor 2
molecules

Inside of
cell

Cell
membrane

Growth factor 1
receptors

2.

Growth
factor 2

Growth
factor 1

Growth factor 1
receptor

3.

Start enzyme
reactions

Cell grows
and divides

molecule, an enzyme, then starts chemical reactions that cause a series of changes in other substances within the cell. The end result can be cell growth and multiplication, differentiation, or even death, depending on the type of cell and the stage of development it has reached.

In 1974, researchers showed that NGF is taken up by the ends of sympathetic or sensory nerve fibers and then conveyed back through the fibers to the cell bodies. Later in the decade, scientists also proved, as Levi-Montalcini had suspected earlier, that NGF directs growing or regenerating fibers of these types of nerves along its concentration gradient. In other words, embryonic tissues destined to receive nerves, such as limbs, produce NGF, and this substance flows back to the spinal cord to guide nerve fibers from the cord to their final destinations. The fibers grow from areas where the NGF concentration is low—that is, near the spinal cord—toward areas where it is higher, in the limbs and other tissues on the borders of the body.

Most thrillingly, Levi-Montalcini's groups and others began to discover in the late 1970s that nerve growth factor affects far more than just nerves. First, they discovered a link between NGF and the adrenal glands, part of the endocrine system. The inner and outer parts of the adrenal glands produce different groups of hormones. Researchers at another laboratory found that when cells from the inner part of such glands were exposed to NGF in tissue culture, they were transformed into cells that strongly resembled sympathetic nerve cells. Similarly, when Levi-Montalcini's group injected NGF into late chick embryos and rat fetuses, the insides of the developing animals' adrenal glands filled up with sympathetic cells instead of the hormone-producing cells that would usually

(Opposite page) *Growth factors, hormones, and other signaling molecules affect cells by combining with other molecules called receptors. (1) Receptor molecules are inserted in the cell membrane, with part of the molecule outside and part inside the cell. The outside of a receptor molecule has a unique shape that fits a particular signaling molecule as a lock fits the key meant to open it. A cell can be affected only by molecules for which it possesses receptors. (2) A growth factor or other signaling molecule begins its action on a cell by attaching, or binding, to the receptors on the cell's surface. Here, molecules of growth factor 1 have bound to their matching receptors, but molecules of growth factor 2 cannot bind because they have the wrong shape for these receptors. (3) After binding, the combined signaling molecules and receptors move inside the cell. There they activate enzymes and start groups of chemical reactions that result in such actions as growth and cell division.*

appear there. These experiments showed that at least one type of hormone-making cell was closely related to nerve cells and could be drastically changed by NGF.

In 1977, Levi-Montalcini's researchers linked NGF to a third major body system: the immune system, which defends the body against attacks by bacteria, viruses, and other foreign substances. They found that injecting NGF into newborn rats produced a striking increase in the number and size of immune system cells called mast cells. These cells are found throughout the body, including the central nervous system and areas close to sensory and sympathetic nerve

Hormones: Long-Distance Signals

Hormones, like growth factors, send signals from one kind of cell to another within the body. They are usually carried from one part of the body to another in liquid form through the blood. All multi-celled organisms, including plants, make hormones. Like nerves, hormones help the different parts of the body work together.

In mammals, most hormones are made by special organs called glands, which together make up a body system known as the endocrine system. Certain substances made by nerves or other tissues, including growth factors such as NGF, are sometimes also classified as hormones because they send signals from cell to cell, even though they do not come from glands.

Each gland makes a different hormone or hormones; some glands make several. For instance, in humans the pituitary gland, a tiny gland buried deep in the brain, makes growth hormone, which produces growth of bones and muscles. This gland, sometimes called the "master gland," also makes hormones that stimulate other glands. When activated by the pituitary hormones, these glands, in turn, produce hormones of their own. The adrenal glands, which sit on top of the kidneys, also produce multiple hormones. Other producers of hormones include the thyroid (a gland in the neck), the testes (in males), and the ovaries (in females).

Hormones are essential for life and health. They play roles in nearly all body functions, including digestion, storage and use of

fibers. Rita Levi-Montalcini wrote in 1997 that "the mast cell can be viewed as a gatekeeper between the immune and nervous systems."

Mast cells play a key part in allergies, in which the immune system reacts to substances (allergens) that are actually harmless but are perceived by the system's cells as dangerous. When mast cells detect substances to which the body has become allergic, they release chemicals that make the tissue around them swell, turn red, and feel painful or itchy. This set of effects, termed inflammation, occurs often when the immune system is activated, as when it fights bacteria that infect a wound. The discovery that NGF could affect mast cells suggested a

energy, and reproduction. If the glands that produce particular hormones are damaged or removed, a person may become ill or even die. For example, cells called beta cells, located within the pancreas, a digestive organ, act as a gland to make the hormone insulin. The body requires insulin to use sugar as an energy source. If the beta cells are damaged or the body becomes unable to respond to insulin, people develop diabetes, a serious illness that can cause death if not treated.

Hormone molecules usually must attach themselves to receptor molecules before they affect cells. Each kind of hormone has its own type or types of receptor. Some receptors are located on the cell's surface, while others are inside the cell. Cells react only to hormones for which they carry receptors.

The actions of hormones are complex. A single hormone can have different effects on different kinds of cells, and the same cell can be affected by more than one hormone. A hormone can stimulate cells to make other hormones or to make more or less of the hormones they are already producing. Hormones can start or stop, or speed up or slow down, chemical reactions within cells. They can change cell membranes in ways that let substances into the cell or block the substances' entry. They can even turn genes on and off (make them active or inactive). Hormones provide a powerful pathway through which a living thing's environment and its genetic programming can interact.

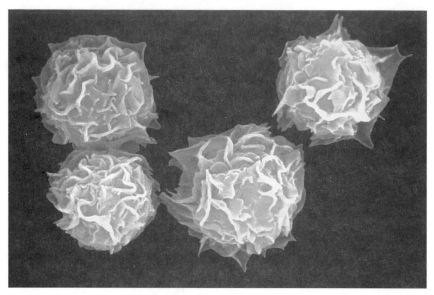

In 1977, Rita Levi-Montalcini's Italian team provided one of the first links between the nervous system and the immune system when they found that nerve growth factor stimulated the multiplication of mast cells, a type of immune cell that is involved in allergy. (Stem Jems/Photo Researchers, Inc.)

connection between the nervous system and the immune system, something that few scientists had considered possible.

Expanding Horizons

In 1977, Rita Levi-Montalcini reached Washington University's mandatory retirement age and finally said good-bye for good to the country she had come to for a "one-semester" visit so long ago. She remained the director of the Laboratory of Cell Biology for two more years, until she arrived at the Italian facility's definition of retirement age as well. By that time, according to Sharon McGrayne, the laboratory had become "one of the largest biological research centers in Italy." Levi-Montalcini had no intention of actually retiring, however. "When you stop working, you are dead," she told Anthony Liversidge of *Omni* magazine in 1988. After her official retirement, she went on working at the laboratory as a "guest" researcher.

Discoveries about NGF and other growth factors snowballed in the 1980s. A 1987 article by Eugene Garfield, editor of *Scientist* magazine, stated that 1,155 papers on NGF alone were published between 1980 and 1987.

Building on information about the sequence of amino acids in NGF, two research teams in the United States identified the gene that carries the code for making the NGF protein in 1983. This gene proved to be virtually identical in mice, chicks, cows, and humans, showing that it had changed very little during the long course of evolution. The same is true of the gene that codes for NGF's receptor on cells. This lack of change suggests that NGF's functions are vital to all vertebrate animals.

Levi-Montalcini's group and others continued to extend scientists' understanding of the range of cells and body systems that NGF could affect. For example, Levi-Montalcini's team showed in 1986 that NGF applied directly to mast cells could make the cells differentiate and show increased function. This discovery greatly increased the evidence for a link between the nervous system and the immune system and "rocked the field," according to Anthony Liversidge, writing in *Omni* magazine in 1988. The group continued to find connections with the endocrine system as well, such as locating NGF receptors on cells from the pituitary and several other glands in rats and showing that NGF could stimulate the glands to make hormones.

Equally startling was researchers' demonstration in 1984 that NGF could affect neurons in the brain as well as in the peripheral nervous system. Using NGF labeled with radioactive tracer atoms, some scientists followed the growth factor's movement from nerve endings in the hippocampus, a part of the brain known to be involved in learning and memory, down nerve fibers to cells in parts of the forebrain. Others showed that a major type of brain neuron, one using the neurotransmitter acetylcholine, responds to NGF by increasing the activity of the enzyme that makes the neurotransmitter. Parts of the brain that proved to be sensitive to NGF include areas that are damaged in mind-destroying illnesses such as Alzheimer's disease and Huntington's disease. Researchers began to wonder whether a lack of NGF might be involved in these conditions and whether a form of NGF might someday provide a treatment for them.

"If You Stop Working, You Are Dead"

On October 13, 1986, when Rita Levi-Montalcini was 77 years old, she received a startling phone call from Sweden. She had won that year's Nobel Prize in physiology or medicine! She was only the fourth woman to win this category of Nobel, and she was the first Italian woman to win the prize in any area of science. She would share the $290,000 award with Stanley Cohen for their work on NGF and other growth factors.

In 1993, Levi-Montalcini told Margaret Holloway, a reporter for *Scientific American,* that she had almost reached the end of an Agatha Christie murder mystery when the phone call came. "I was very happy" about the news, Levi-Montalcini recalled, "but I wanted much more to know the end of the story" she had been reading.

In her autobiography, strangely, Levi-Montalcini did not say that the world-famous prize had been awarded to her. Instead, she fantasized that it was given to nerve growth factor itself, "whom" she pictured as the same haunting figure she had first glimpsed in Brazil.

> *It was in the anticipatory, pre-Carnival atmosphere of Rio de Janeiro that in 1952 NGF lifted its mask to reveal its miraculous ability to cause the growth, in the space of a few hours, of dense auras of nervous fibers. Thus began its saga.*
>
> *On Christmas Eve 1986, NGF appeared in public under large floodlights, . . . in the presence of the royals of Sweden. . . . Wrapped in a black mantle [as Levi-Montalcini herself was at the award ceremony], he bowed before the king and, for a moment, lowered the veil covering his face. We recognized each other in a matter of seconds when I saw him looking for me among the applauding crowd. He then replaced his veil and disappeared as suddenly as he had appeared. . . . Will we see each other again? Or was that instant the fulfillment of my desire of many years to meet him, and I have henceforth lost trace of him forever?*

Flood of Honors

Most scientists thought that Levi-Montalcini's Nobel Prize was well earned, but the award did arouse a certain amount of controversy. At the time the prize was given, some researchers expressed the feeling that Viktor Hamburger as well as Levi-Montalcini and Cohen should have been honored. (Up to three people can share a single prize.) Hamburger's work in the 1920s, 1930s, and 1940s, they said, prepared the way for the later discoveries that Levi-Montalcini and Cohen made. Levi-Montalcini did not agree, however. "Viktor Hamburger was not there [in Brazil] when I made the discovery of . . . NGF," she said in her 1988 *Omni* magazine interview. "He had no participation in this."

In early September 1995, furthermore, the Swedish newspaper *Dagens Nyheter*, which a *Science* magazine article called "the country's most influential newspaper," caused a stir by claiming that Fidia, an Italian pharmaceutical company, had pressured the Nobel committee to give the 1986 prize to Levi-Montalcini.

Fidia had funded Levi-Montalcini's research at the Center of Neurobiology in Rome during the 1980s, after her official retirement, because the company was looking for treatments for neurodegenerative diseases such as Alzheimer's disease and hoped that her work might lead to such drugs. The newspaper alleged that the drug firm had given gifts and prizes to committee members in what the paper termed a "gigantic campaign." After protests by the scientific community and the Nobel committee, however, *Dagens Nyheter* issued a partial retraction of its accusation in an editorial on September 15. It said it had never meant to claim that the committee had been bribed, and it did not question Levi-Montalcini's worthiness to receive the award.

The flood of honors that Levi-Montalcini received in the 1980s certainly indicated that the Nobel committee was far from alone in its regard for her. In 1983, for example, she shared Columbia University's Louisa Gross Horwitz Prize with Stanley Cohen and Viktor Hamburger. On September 22, 1986, just a few weeks before she won the Nobel Prize, she received the $15,000 Albert Lasker Award for Basic Medical Research, which she also shared with Stanley Cohen. This award, which Ruby Rohrlich's article about Levi-Montalcini in *Judaism* termed "the most prestigious science prize in the United States," is often considered a prelude to a medicine Nobel. Levi-Montalcini also received the National Medal of Science, the highest scientific award given by the U.S. government, in 1987, and she was the first woman to be admitted to Italy's Pontifical Academy of Sciences.

An Active Life

In 1988, Rita Levi-Montalcini published her autobiography, *In Praise of Imperfection*. Reviews of the book were mixed. For example, Dale Purves, writing for *Science* magazine, complained that Levi-Montalcini had presented "a superficial and fairy-tale view of science and how it is accomplished." Purves also claimed that she had not given enough credit to Giuseppe Levi, Viktor Hamburger, and Pietro Angeletti for their contributions to her research.

Levi-Montalcini later wrote other books as well. She edited *The Saga of the Nerve Growth Factor,* an anthology of key scientific papers on this subject by herself and others, which was published in 1997. In 1999, following a gala public celebration of her 90th birthday on April 22, she published *Ninety Years in the Galaxy of the Mind,* which described her continuing research on the brain and presented a system of ethics for future generations. Her other books include *Cantico di una vita* (Song of a life), a series of about 200 letters written to her mother during the years she made her key discoveries, which appeared in 2001. Of these books, only *In Praise of Imperfection* and *The Saga of the Nerve Growth Factor* have been translated into English. As of 2000, Levi-Montalcini had also written more than 200 scientific papers, several articles on the social significance of science, and a paper on the women's emancipation movement from the early 19th century to 1970.

In her 90s, Levi-Montalcini no longer does laboratory work because of poor vision. She continues to maintain a connection with her laboratory, however; her name appeared on a scientific paper (about production of recombinant human nerve growth factor for potential use as a drug) as recently as December 2005. She still leads an active life in other ways as well. She was made a life member of the Italian Senate in 2001 and was still attending Senate meetings in 2006, when she was the oldest member of that body. She is now the last surviving member of her generation in her family: Gino died of a heart attack in 1974, Paola passed away in September 2000, and Anna followed soon after.

Levi-Montalcini founded the European Brain Research Institute (EBRI) in Rome in the early 2000s. According to the institute's Web site, its mission is "the study of the central nervous system, from the neurons to the whole brain, in health and diseases." It focuses on research aimed at understanding neurological, and especially neuro-degenerative, diseases such as Alzheimer's, Parkinson's, Huntington's, and ALS ("Lou Gehrig's disease," an illness of unknown cause that produces progressively worsening neuromuscular weakness).

Levi-Montalcini and her twin sister also established the Rita Levi-Montalcini Onlus Foundation in the early 1990s. This foundation, funded with Levi-Montalcini's life savings, provides scholarships and fellowships to educate young women in Africa. Its first beneficiaries were in Ethiopia; an article in the November 21, 2004, *St. Louis Post-Dispatch* said that Levi-Montalcini saw a link between the discrimination she had suffered earlier as a Jew in Italy and the way girls and women were discriminated against in that country. By 2004, the article said, the foundation had helped more than 200 African women reach such goals as attending medical school. Manlio Dell'Ariccia, the country director for Ethiopia at the American Jewish Joint Distribution Committee, who helped Levi-Montalcini implement her work there, said that the Nobel laureate would be remembered for "her personal humanity and deep involvement in improving living conditions of the poorest" as well as for her scientific achievements.

This foundation is Levi-Montalcini's chief charitable work, but it certainly has not been her only one. In the 1990s she was president of the Italian Association for Multiple Sclerosis, a disease that NGF, ironically, makes worse. With Roman sociologist Eleonora Barbiere Masini and others, she formed the Women's International Network for Emergency and Solidarity (WIN) in 1995. This group, with support from the European Union and the United Nations Educational, Scientific and Cultural Organization (UNESCO), published a directory of organizations that women could contact to obtain help with problems such as domestic abuse, debt, and forced prostitution. Levi-Montalcini was also one

Rita Levi-Montalcini has remained active well into her 90s. She is shown here in 1997. (Associated Press)

of four special ambassadors chosen by the United Nations Food and Agriculture Organization (FAO) for World Food Day in 1999. She often spoke to teenagers in schools, encouraging them to have faith in people and in the possibility of peace.

The Links Strengthen

Rita Levi-Montalcini first proposed in a paper in 1990 that nerve growth factor is a key link between the nervous system, the endocrine system, and the immune system. Many pieces of evidence obtained in different laboratories since then have supported her claim. This substance appears to be an essential part of the body's efforts to maintain its health, respond to its environment, and protect itself.

To begin with, Levi-Montalcini's Italian team and others have continued to establish connections between NGF and the immune system. In 1994, Levi-Montalcini's laboratory showed that mast cells make, store, and release NGF, and other researchers proved that these cells have receptors to the factor on their surfaces. Mast cells, furthermore, have turned out to be not the only parts of the immune system that respond to NGF. Several types of white blood cells, key players in the immune system, produce NGF, have receptors for it on their surfaces, or both. Indeed, scientists in the early 1990s found that NGF can cause most types of cells in the blood to multiply. NGF interacts in complex ways with other chemicals produced by the immune system to intensify or reduce the system's reactions to substances from the environment that come into contact with the body.

Bacteria, viruses, and allergens are far from the only kinds of danger that humans and animals face, and the immune system is not the body's only tool for defending itself; the nervous system acts to fend off threats as well. The brain reacts to danger by generating emotions such as fear and anger and by signaling glands in the endocrine system to release a flood of hormones that prepare the body for "fight or flight." Scientists, including some in Levi-Montalcini's laboratory, have found that NGF is intimately involved in the nervous system's responses to stress. Speaking in human terms, Richard Lazarus, a professor of psychology at the University of California, Berkeley, and Susan Folkman defined stress as "a particular relationship between the person and the environment that is appraised by the person as taxing or exceeding his or her resources and endangering his or her well-being."

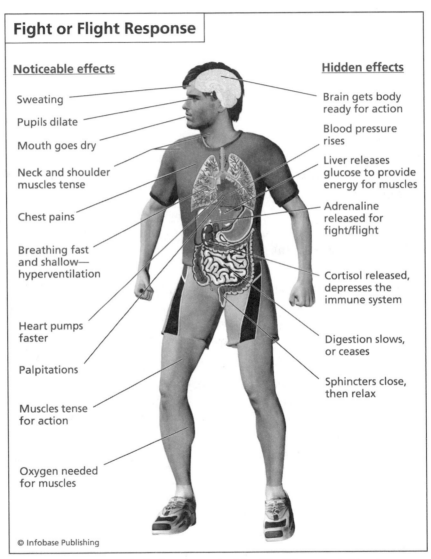

Fight or Flight Response

Noticeable effects

Sweating

Pupils dilate

Mouth goes dry

Neck and shoulder muscles tense

Chest pains

Breathing fast and shallow— hyperventilation

Heart pumps faster

Palpitations

Muscles tense for action

Oxygen needed for muscles

Hidden effects

Brain gets body ready for action

Blood pressure rises

Liver releases glucose to provide energy for muscles

Adrenaline released for fight/flight

Cortisol released, depresses the immune system

Digestion slows, or ceases

Sphincters close, then relax

© Infobase Publishing

When faced with stress, the body prepares to defend itself through what has been termed a "fight or flight" reaction. The reaction starts in the nervous system, then spreads to the endocrine or glandular system (whose hormones produce many of the effects shown here) and the immune system. Rita Levi-Montalcini and others showed in the 1990s that nerve growth factor is intimately involved in coordinating these systems' responses to danger.

Levi-Montalcini's team found perhaps the first connection between NGF and reactions to stress in the late 1980s when they returned to male mice, whose salivary glands had proven to be such a rich source of NGF for Levi-Montalcini and Stanley Cohen in the 1950s. They found that when they made the mice fight, NGF levels increased not only in the animals' salivary glands but in their bloodstream and their hypothalamus, which was already known to be involved in stress reactions and the body's defense. The hypothalamus receives input from the senses and from other parts of the nervous system that monitor the condition of the body. When it detects conditions that are dangerously outside an animal's normal range, it sends signals to other nerves that control such things as blood pressure and heart rate. It also triggers the pituitary gland to order other glands to produce hormones that ready the body for action. Levi-Montalcini and her coworkers concluded that the release of NGF not only is triggered by, but helps to shape, the mice's fighting behavior. Drawing on this and other research, Levi-Montalcini stated in 1997 that NGF probably plays an "alerting role" in processes involved in helping the body defend itself and maintain its normal condition.

Researchers have found that NGF plays a role in human emotions and reactions to stress, too. As early as 1994, Levi-Montalcini reported in *The Saga of the Nerve Growth Factor*, levels of NGF in people's blood were shown to increase both just before and just after events that made the people feel anxious or stressed. More recently, a Japanese scientist reported that even the minor stress of composing e-mail on a cell phone raised blood levels of NGF and related substances, as well as the severity of allergic reactions, in people with a certain type of skin allergy. Laughter (produced by watching a humorous video), on the other hand, lowered the levels of NGF in the people's blood and prevented the rise associated with the cell phone activity. Laughter also reduced the intensity of their allergic reactions.

Even the "good stress" of romantic love increases NGF levels, Italian researchers (not associated with Levi-Montalcini) reported in 2005. Enzo Emanuele and his coworkers measured levels of NGF in the blood of 58 people between the ages of 18 and 31 who said they had recently fallen in love. NGF levels were significantly higher in the romantics than in people of a similar age who either were not in a relationship or were involved in a long-term relationship that had started years previously, Emanuele said. Among the newly in love group, the people who expressed the strongest feelings had the highest levels of the growth factor. Emanuele added that levels of NGF fell back to normal after about a year, even if the new relationships continued. This did not mean that the people no longer loved each other, his team thought, but merely that NGF is most important at

Psychoneuroimmunology: Connecting Mind and Body

Rita Levi-Montalcini was far from the only, or even the first, scientist to find links between the nervous system, the immune system, and the endocrine system or to suggest that these systems work together to respond to stress. Near the beginning of the 20th century, Walter Cannon, a professor of physiology at Harvard University, found that strong emotions in animals, such as fear and rage, produced physical effects on the stomach, partly through actions of sympathetic nerves, the type that Levi-Montalcini would later show are strongly affected by NGF.

A Canadian endocrinologist, Hans Selye, reported in 1936 that animals react to stress through changes in the pituitary, adrenals, and other endocrine glands and in the amounts of hormones they produce. These changes, in turn, are triggered by a part of the brain called the hypothalamus. If the stress continues long enough, this reaction can damage the body in various ways and even cause death. Selye later showed that, in humans, strong positive emotions or experiences can be just as stressful as negative ones.

The immune system was first brought into this picture in 1964 when George F. Solomon, a professor of psychiatry and biobehavioral sciences at the University of California, Los Angeles, demonstrated weakened immune systems in mental patients. Robert Ader and Nicholas Cohen at the University of Rochester, New York, formally presented the theory that psychological reactions could affect the immune system in 1975 and gave the study of this topic the name *psychoneuroimmunology.*

the beginning of a relationship, when a bond is being formed and the body is "on alert" that something exciting is happening.

NGF may well be involved, not only in learning to love someone, but in learning in general. Although scientists have traditionally said that people are born with all the nerve cells they will ever have, researchers have learned in the past two decades that adult brains can change themselves considerably by forming new connections between cells. This ability has allowed some people to regain body

Two years later, Rita Levi-Montalcini provided one of the first hints of a mechanism through which the nervous and immune systems might interact when she found indirect evidence that nerve growth factor, which primarily affects nerves, could also act on one type of cell in the immune system, the mast cell. This connection was strengthened in 1981 when David Felten, then at Indiana University, showed clusters of nerve endings in organs where mast cells and other immune system cells are produced.

Candace Pert, a scientist then at the National Institute of Mental Health, part of the National Institutes of Health in Bethesda, Maryland, showed in the early 1980s that receptors for small protein molecules called neuropeptides exist on certain cells in the immune system as well as certain brain cells—the first direct evidence of a means by which cells in these two systems could communicate with one another. Levi-Montalcini demonstrated a second such mechanism shortly afterward when she showed that NGF directly affects both mast cells and cells in glands such as the pituitary.

Since that time, evidence for links between the brain and nervous system, the immune system, and the endocrine system has multiplied. Cells in all these systems produce and react to many of the same signaling molecules. As more is learned about these connections, they are bound to have a powerful effect on medicine. Researchers remain unsure, however, about the exact relationship between emotions and disease in humans and about how to apply what has been learned about this relationship to cure illness or preserve health.

Xiaolin He (left) and Chris Garcia of Stanford University School of Medicine are among the young scientists following in Rita Levi-Montalcini's footsteps by studying nerve growth factor. They used a combination of X-ray imaging techniques and biochemical methods to work out the three-dimensional structure of the molecule formed when NGF binds to the two types of receptors that can accept it. Understanding NGF's inter- action with receptors may be helpful in turning the growth factor into a drug that can treat Alzheimer's disease or other serious conditions. (Mitzi Baker/Stanford University School of Medicine)

functions even after events such as strokes or severe head injuries. Levi-Montalcini and some other scientists have suspected at least since 1989, when researchers showed that NGF made new fibers sprout from the ends of brain neurons in adult rats and mice, that this growth factor may play a part in the great flexibility of structure and function that adults' brains have been shown to possess.

In 2001, researchers at the University of Rochester Medical Center in New York found further evidence for this idea. Using genetic engineering, Howard Federoff's laboratory modified a group of laboratory mice so that nerve cells in their hippocampus contained extra genes for making NGF. Cells in this brain area, which is crucial for memory and learning, normally make NGF and send it through their fibers to a second area, the basal forebrain, where the growth factor makes new nerve connections sprout. The added genes made the altered mice able to make more NGF than other mice.

After the treatment, Federoff divided the engineered mice, and some untreated mice as well, into three groups. One group simply moved around their cages as they wished. A second group ran the same maze day after day or performed other repetitive tasks. The third group was constantly challenged with new mazes and other learning experiences. After eight months, about half the adult life of a mouse, the animals that had both extra NGF and challenging learning experiences were able to learn new mazes much more quickly than mice that lacked either the growth factor or the learning practice. The neurons in the basal forebrains of these mice were also about 60 percent larger than those in the other mice, and they had more than three times as many neurons connecting the forebrain and the hippocampus. These results strongly suggest that NGF plays a part in the rewiring of the brain that is involved in learning.

Nerve Growth Factor in Health and Disease

Nerve growth factor may be involved in certain diseases as well as in maintaining health. Inflammation, a normal part of the immune system's attempts to defend the body, produces pain, redness, swelling, and other unpleasant effects. Levi-Montalcini and others showed that NGF increases rapidly in inflamed areas and plays a major role in inflammation through its effects on mast cells and other immune system cells. In the early 1990s, Levi-Montalcini's team went on to demonstrate that this growth factor is particularly involved in the pain of inflammation. It does not cause pain directly, Levi-Montalcini wrote in *The Saga of the Nerve Growth Factor,* but rather makes nerve endings in the inflamed area more sensitive to pressure and heat. This occurs not only in normal inflammation but also in rheumatoid arthritis and other so-called autoimmune diseases, in which the immune system mistakenly attacks parts of a person's own body.

Some scientists hope to turn this knowledge of NGF's involvement in the pain of inflammation into a new kind of pain-fighting drug. Narcotics used to control pain can cause addiction, and other painkillers, including many used to treat arthritis, have proven to increase the risk of bleeding, heart attacks, and other problems. A painkiller that works through a new mechanism might therefore be very valuable. Genentech, the first company to make medicines with genetic engineering, and a smaller biotechnology company called Rinat (now part of Pfizer, a large drug firm) worked together in 2004 to test a drug called RI 624, which was an antibody to NGF. This drug was expected to reduce pain connected with inflammation, and possibly other conditions, including cancer, by blocking the action of NGF.

NGF itself may also have a future as a drug. The most exciting possibilities for its use are as treatments for illnesses that destroy neurons in parts of the brain, including Alzheimer's disease, Parkinson's disease, and Huntington's disease. Alzheimer's disease is the most common cause of dementia, or extreme mental confusion, in humans. According to the Alzheimer's Association, the disease affects more than 5 million people, mostly elderly, in the United States alone. It destroys neurons in the hippocampus and other parts of the brain involved in thinking, memory, and learning, and no effective treatment for it is currently known. Parkinson's disease primarily affects movement, though it can cause difficulties with thinking as well. Huntington's disease, a rare but deadly illness caused by a defective gene, produces both dementia and difficulties in movement.

All three of these so-called neurodegenerative diseases affect types of neurons that have been shown to produce NGF, respond to this growth factor, or both. Therefore, medical researchers and biotechnology companies have hoped that giving patients NGF, or perhaps increasing their own production of the growth factor by, for instance, transplanting the gene for NGF into their brains, might restore brain function to people suffering from these conditions. Supporting this hope, scientists found in 2000 that infusing NGF into the brains of elderly rats with memory and learning impairments improved their memory and seemed to prevent the death of certain neurons.

Mark Tuszynski and other researchers, working at the University of California, San Diego, transplanted skin cells genetically modified to produce NGF into the forebrain of an Alzheimer's patient in 2001. The cells had been taken from the patient's own skin and modified in the laboratory. This experiment, the first attempt at gene therapy (use of inserted genes to treat illness) to treat Alzheimer's disease, earned Tuszynski the Kappers Award, an international award for brain research, in that year.

A later report on Tuszynski's work, published in 2005, stated that in six people with mild to moderate Alzheimer's disease, his treatment slowed the rate of progression of the disease by 36 to 51 percent. Brain scans showed increased metabolism, a sign of improved neuron health, in the treated areas. A second small trial, using an improved method of inserting the altered genes, began in 2005 but had not been evaluated as of January 2008, when Tuszynski's laboratory issued its most recent report. This report stated that a larger trial of the treatment was scheduled to begin later in 2008. Tuszynski's group is also examining the roles that NGF and other growth factors might play in repairing spinal cord injury and in helping the brain develop new connections.

Growth Factors and Cancer

Scientists have also continued to study epidermal growth factor and other growth factors in addition to NGF. Dozens of such factors have now been identified and grouped into "families" of compounds with similar actions and chemical structure.

Perhaps the most exciting discovery about growth factors has been that some of them are powerfully linked with cancer. Research that led to this discovery began in the 1970s, when a number of scientists studied viruses known to cause cancer in animals. They found that certain cancer-causing viruses possessed genes that related viruses unable to cause cancer lacked. Robert Huebner and George Todaro of the National Cancer Institute, part of the government-sponsored National Institutes of Health, gave these genes the name *oncogenes,* after a Greek word meaning "cancer."

In 1976, J. Michael Bishop, Harold Varmus, and their coworkers at the University of California, San Francisco, made a startling discovery: A gene almost identical to an oncogene called *src,* which had come from a virus that causes cancer in chickens, also existed in normal chicken cells. Bishop and Varmus concluded that oncogenes might not really be virus genes at all. Instead, they appeared to be normal cell genes that the viruses had picked up from the genomes of cells they infected and added to their own. Over time, the genes had become mutated in ways that made them cause cancer when the viruses reinserted them into cells. This theory was shown to be correct in the early 1980s, when normal forms of many other oncogenes were identified. Bishop and Varmus were awarded the Nobel Prize in physiology or medicine for their idea in 1989.

Cancer is a condition in which cells grow and multiply uncontrollably, so it was not surprising that most oncogenes proved to be distorted forms of genes connected with cell reproduction and growth. Several of them turned out to be forms of genes that carry the code for growth factors or growth factor receptors. The first oncogene to be linked to growth factors was one called *erbB*, which scientists identified in 1984 as a mutated gene for the epidermal growth factor receptor. Another oncogene, *HER-2*, which is associated with some cases of human breast cancer, has also proved to be an altered EGF receptor gene. These genes may make extra copies of the receptor, which would make cells more susceptible to the action of EGF. Alternatively, they may make the cells produce the receptor at times when they should not do so, or they may produce a form of the receptor that interacts with EGF and other cell substances in an abnormal way. In any case, the result is cells that grow and multiply much more than they should.

Another growth factor, called vascular endothelial growth factor or VEGF, is involved in cancer in a different way. VEGF's normal job in the body is making new blood vessels grow, a process called angiogenesis. Cancerous tumors, like healthy organs and tissues, need blood vessels to bring them oxygen and carry away their waste products. Cancer cells produce VEGF to obtain the vessels they need. Nerve growth factor may also contribute to tumor-produced angiogenesis.

Harold Dvorak of Harvard Medical School found the link between cancer and VEGF in 1983. Long before then—in the 1960s—another researcher at the same institution, Judah Folkman, noticed that cancers needed a blood supply in order to survive and

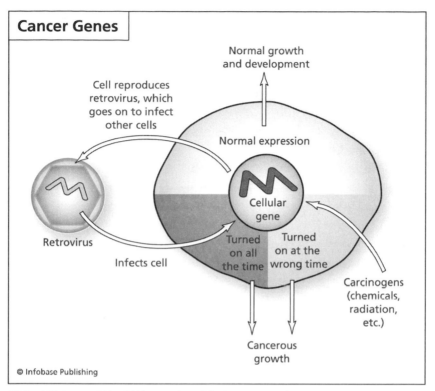

Cancer Genes

Michael Bishop and Harold Varmus found that cancer-causing genes, or oncogenes, were originally normal genes, such as genes that carry the code for growth factors or their receptors. Sometimes retroviruses accidentally captured these genes when the viruses infected cells. Long afterward, other retroviruses carrying the genes can trigger cancer when they infect new cells and insert the genes back into the cells' genomes. Alternatively, carcinogens (cancer-causing chemicals) can produce mutations that change a normal cell gene to an oncogene. Oncogenes differ from the normal form of the same genes in that the oncogenes either produce their proteins all the time or produce them at the wrong time in the cells' life cycle.

suggested attacking tumors by blocking their ability to carry out angiogenesis. Folkman's laboratory discovered two angiogenesis inhibitors and began testing them on mice as anticancer drugs in the mid-1990s. Since then, a number of angiogenesis inhibitors have been approved to treat advanced cancer in humans. Several, including Avastin (bevacizumab), the first such drug to gain approval from the FDA (in 2004), block the action of VEGF in one way or another.

Researchers hope that drugs like Avastin and others that block epidermal growth factor or its receptor, such as Herceptin—so-called biologics—will be more effective and less harmful to patients than classic chemotherapy drugs because they target particular cell activities related to cancer rather than simply poisoning whole cells. "Because [growth factor inhibitors] target the source of the disease rather than eliminating its side effects, there is potential for them to be curative," an article in the May 2004 *Manufacturing Chemist* stated.

VEGF is involved in other diseases besides cancer, including diabetic retinopathy and the wet form of age-related macular degeneration. Both of these illnesses involve abnormal blood vessels forming inside the eye and can lead to blindness. Diabetic retinopathy is a complication of diabetes; age-related macular degeneration's cause is unknown, but it is the leading cause of blindness in older people in industrialized countries. Several of the drugs used to treat wet age-related macular degeneration are inhibitors of VEGF.

A Turning Point in Medicine

On the other hand, VEGF and other growth factors have been studied as possible medical treatments or even approved for use as drugs. Researchers have experimented with VEGF as a treatment for diabetic neuropathy, in which people with diabetes lose sensation in their arms and legs because of poor blood circulation, and for forms of heart disease in which the heart muscle is starved for blood because circulation in the arteries that normally feed it are blocked. NGF has also been used, at least in animals, to treat conditions stemming from lack of functioning blood vessels.

Stanley Cohen's epidermal growth factor has been used as a medication since before Cohen won his Nobel Prize. It speeds healing of wounds in eyes and skin, makes transplants of corneas (the clear outer covering of the eye) more likely to succeed, and produces rapid laboratory growth of skin to be used on burn victims. NGF and "cocktails" containing a mixture of growth factors have also been used to treat some hard-to-heal wounds, such as diabetic ulcers and pressure ulcers (bedsores). A mixture of 16 growth factors and related compounds involved in wound healing was even being tested in 2007 as a skin cream to remove wrinkles and other signs of age.

The possibilities of NGF and other growth factors in medicine seem endless. As Carol Kahn wrote in an article about them in *Omni* magazine in March 1988:

> *Human growth factors represent a turning point in medicine. . . . With the ability to produce growth factors . . . through genetic engineering, we have entered a new era, in which the products of our own body can be harvested to make up for nature's deficiencies and even manipulated to improve on the original plan. When we become the source of our own healing, we will have engendered the most powerful medicine of all.*

If that day comes, the people who benefit from the healing power of growth factors will owe much to the intuition, persistence, and courage of Rita Levi-Montalcini.

Conclusion:

Answering Many Questions

A press release issued by the Nobel committee when Rita Levi-Montalcini and Stanley Cohen won the 1986 prize in physiology or medicine stated that their work "opened new fields of widespread importance to basic science." The speaker who awarded the prizes mentioned that it was "of potential importance to future medicine" as well. Alexander Grimwade, then director of the division of the Institute for Scientific Information that produced a yearly *Atlas of Science,* stated shortly afterward that "at least 20 distinct areas of research . . . owe a heavy debt to Cohen and Levi-Montalcini's work."

In the late 2000s, that estimate would be far higher. Researchers, including Levi-Montalcini herself, have now revealed connections between growth factors and other aspects of the body's development and maintenance that were undreamed of, or just beginning to be glimpsed, at the time Levi-Montalcini and Cohen accepted their awards. In fact, these signaling substances appear to be part of the answers to some of the most important questions in biology.

Guiding Growth

How do living things develop? Curiosity about the way humans and animals develop before birth led Levi-Montalcini to begin her scientific investigations as the bombs of war fell around her. She hoped to reveal at least a tiny part of the answer to the fundamental question of how a single cell can develop into the many types of tissue, organized in infinitely complex ways, that make up a living organism. In particular, she wanted to understand the development of the nervous system, through which animals interact with their environment. Her work ultimately revealed one of the key forces that guides and controls this complicated process. As Kerstin Hall of the Karolinska Institute put it in the presentation speech for Levi-Montalcini's Nobel Prize,

> *The discovery, identification and isolation of NGF created a breakthrough in the research field of developmental neurobiology. . . . The neurotropic [nerve-attracting] effect of NGF offers an explanation of how nerve fibers can find their way through the tangle of nerves in the [developing] brain.*

Even more important, Levi-Montalcini's discovery of NGF revealed a whole new class of biomolecules that have proven to play a major part in the body's growth and development. "The discovery of growth factors . . . led to a new understanding—growth and differentiation are regulated by signal substances released from cells and acting on neighboring cells," Kerstin Hall stated in his Nobel Prize presentation speech. The discovery of NGF and epidermal growth factor, which Stanley Cohen found after he left Levi-Montalcini's laboratory, "initiated a new era in the research area of growth and differentiation."

Does the nervous system stay the same or change? In fact, NGF's role in embryonic development turned out to be just the first example of its importance. Levi-Montalcini went on to show that this substance is essential for the health of certain types of nerve cells in adult animals as well. Her work, and that of other scientists who built on it, has revealed that the nervous system is constantly changing, not only in unborn animals and humans, but in those that are fully mature. This new appreciation of the system's dynamic qualities has underscored the recognition that new learning can take place throughout life. It also offers hope for potential recovery even from the devastating nerve cell damage caused by conditions such as stroke and spinal cord injury.

Apoptosis: Death as a Part of Life

Cells must die, just as whole living things must. They can die in one of two ways. The first way, called necrosis, occurs when cells are mechanically damaged or are poisoned by toxins. In essence, these cells are murdered. They break open and attract the attention of the immune system (the body's police force), causing inflammation and other immune reactions.

The second form of cell death is apoptosis, or programmed cell death. In this case, signals from outside or inside tell the cell that it needs to die, and the cell essentially commits suicide. It begins a series of chemical reactions that destroy key parts of itself, including the cytoskeleton that holds it together and the DNA that carries its genetic instructions. Its membrane bubbles and blisters but does not break. It shrinks down and is eventually vacuumed away by macrophages, the body's garbage collectors.

As Rita Levi-Montalcini first observed in her bedroom hideaway in war-torn Italy, programmed cell death is a normal part of development. An embryo's nervous system, for example, creates far more neurons than it needs. While some neurons migrate to their final places in the emerging system, the body marks others as unnecessary and tells them to die. Similarly, a human embryo's hands and feet begin as solid pieces, like mittens. The fingers and toes separate when genetic signals tell the cells of the tissue between them to die.

The body also protects itself by ordering certain cells to die. For instance, immune system cells multiply in order to destroy invading bacteria or viruses. After that battle is over, the body has far more

Coordinating Defense

How does the body preserve and defend itself? Levi-Montalcini and other scientists studying NGF showed in the 1980s and beyond that this biochemical provides a link between three of the most important systems in the body: the nervous system, the endocrine system, and the immune system. Their research was among the first to reveal this connection and offer a mechanism by which these vital systems could communicate with one another. They showed a way

of these cells than it needs. If left alive, these restless "soldiers" might turn their weapons on the body itself. To prevent this, most of these cells are told to undergo apoptosis. In another protective form of apoptosis, certain immune system cells attach themselves to other cells that have been infected by viruses and signal those cells to begin a self-destruction program.

Stress within the cell can trigger apoptosis, too. Rita Levi-Montalcini showed that if certain types of nerve cells do not receive regular stimulation from nerve growth factor, they begin apoptosis. Other types of cells respond in the same way to the loss of other growth factors. Certain kinds of cell damage, such as harm to cells' DNA or formation of abnormal proteins, can also turn on the death program. If protective genes called tumor suppressor genes detect changes that mean a cell is becoming cancerous, they order the cell to kill itself.

When apoptosis fails to occur at the right time, or occurs at the wrong one, illness can arise. Malignant tumors may form when tumor suppressor genes become damaged or inactivated, for instance. On the other hand, healthy neurons are wrongly condemned to death in neurodegenerative diseases such as Alzheimer's disease. Part of the loss of immune system cells that occurs in AIDS also seems to come through incorrectly triggered apoptosis.

Normal apoptosis, however, is a sign of health. In an individual organism's body, just as in a larger ecological system, death is a necessary part of life.

in which thoughts and emotions could affect the body's reactions and physical health.

As Levi-Montalcini emphasized in her 1997 book, *The Saga of the Nerve Growth Factor*, NGF plays a central role in what has come to be called homeostasis—the body's mechanisms for maintaining and protecting itself in the face of the stresses presented by a constantly changing environment. She concluded at that time that NGF acts as an "alerting" signal, warning the body that potentially dangerous conditions have been detected. This substance helps to unify and manage the defense operations mounted by the brain and nerves, the cells of the immune system, and the endocrine system's many hormones. "NGF is . . . beginning to emerge as a crucial coordinator of the body's major homeostatic systems and defense strategies," she wrote. Research since that time has confirmed her belief.

How do cells communicate? The study of NGF and other growth factors has led to a new understanding of the way that cells send signals to one another and respond to signals that they receive. It has helped to reveal the complex chain of events that begins when a growth factor, hormone, or other signaling molecule attaches to a receptor on the surface of a cell. It has shown how the chemical reactions triggered by these signaling molecules can turn genes on and off and make a cell grow, divide, or die. Signaling molecules have proved to be a key path through which organisms' genetic programming interacts with their environment.

What parts do cell growth and death play in the life of the body? Growth factors have proved to be involved in the lives of cells, and of the body as a whole, from conception to death. As their name suggests, they trigger cell growth—both the normal growth that takes place in a healthy body and the abnormal, uncontrollable growth of cancer. They also help cells and bodies repair and maintain themselves.

On the other hand, growth factors, or sometimes their absence, can cause the destruction of cells. This cell death may be the result of a disease process or of the deterioration brought about by aging. As Levi-Montalcini was one of the first to recognize, however, it can also be part of a protective mechanism—certain genes can order cancer cells to kill themselves, for instance—or of normal development. When Levi-Montalcini observed masses of neurons dying in her chick embryos in 1947, she realized that she was seeing a necessary stage in the maturing of the nervous system. Most other scientists did not understand until the 1970s that similar programmed cell death plays a part in the development and maintenance of all the body's systems.

Protecting against Disease

How can basic science contribute to medicine? Rita Levi-Montalcini's research has done more than help scientists understand how the body develops, maintains itself, and responds to change. It also offers new hope for people suffering from terrible diseases. Nerve growth factor has not yet found a major use as a drug, but researchers continue to investigate the possibility that it may be able to protect or restore the neurons of patients with such conditions as Alzheimer's disease and Parkinson's disease. Other growth factors have proved useful for healing wounds, restoring parts of the immune system, and creating new blood vessels in areas where the original vessels have become blocked. Drugs that stop the action of certain growth factors, on the other hand, now help to fight cancer and several serious eye diseases. Many thousands of people owe their restored health or even their lives to the discoveries that began so long ago in this brave woman's "Robinson Crusoe" home laboratory.

CHRONOLOGY

1873	Camilo Golgi invents a stain that shows nerve cells clearly for the first time.
April 22, 1909	Rita Levi-Montalcini is born in Turin, Italy.
1925	Fascist leader Benito Mussolini becomes dictator of Italy.
1930	Levi-Montalcini enters Turin University's medical school.
1932–1936	Is an intern in the laboratory of Giuseppe Levi
1936	Earns her medical degree with top honors
1936–1938	Treats patients and does research with Fabio Visintini at Turin University
November 1938	Loses her university job because of a new law that forbids all teaching jobs to Jews
1939	Works at the Neurologic Institute in Brussels, Belgium, from March to November; returns to Italy in December after World War II begins
June 10, 1940	Italy enters World War II on the side of Germany.
1940–1941	Levi-Montalcini duplicates Viktor Hamburger's experiments on the nervous system of chick embryos in a home laboratory.

1942	Levi-Montalcini's family moves out of Turin to escape bombing; she continues her experiments.
1943	Mussolini resigns on July 25; Italy withdraws from the war on September 8; Germany invades Italy on September 9 and establishes a puppet state in northern Italy.
October 1943– September 1944	Levi-Montalcini and her family live under assumed names in Florence to avoid German persecution of Italian Jews.
September 1944– May 1945	Works as a volunteer physician for the Allied Health Service
May 2, 1945	German troops in Italy surrender to the Allies.
July 1945	Levi-Montalcini's family return to Turin; she resumes her post at Turin University.
September 1946	Goes to the United States to work with Viktor Hamburger at Washington University in St. Louis
1947	Repeats her earlier work on nerve development in chick embryos and proves that her conclusions rather than Hamburger's were correct; realizes that cell migration and death play an important part in the nervous system's development
1950–1951	Repeats Elmer Bueker's experiments with mouse tumors grafted onto chick embryos and obtains striking nerve growth; concludes that the growth is stimulated by a liquid released from the tumors; describes this factor at a meeting of the New York Academy of Sciences

September–November 1952	Working in Rio de Janeiro, Brazil, Levi-Montalcini shows that the tumors' growth effect works on nerves grown in tissue culture as well as in whole embryos.
January 1953	Returns to St. Louis and begins working with Stanley Cohen
1956	Levi-Montalcini and Cohen discover that nerve growth factor (NGF) is a protein and is present in snake venom; Levi-Montalcini becomes a U.S. citizen.
1956–1958	Shows that NGF from snake venom produces nerve growth in both whole embryos and cultured tissue; Cohen determines the molecular weight of NGF
1958	Levi-Montalcini and Cohen find large quantities of NGF in the salivary glands of male mice; Levi-Montalcini becomes a full professor at Washington University.
June 11, 1959	Learns that blocking the action of NGF in newborn mice and rats completely prevents the development of their sympathetic nervous system
July 1959	Cohen ends his collaboration with Levi-Montalcini and leaves Washington University.
1961	Sets up a small research unit in Rome and begins spending part of each year in Italy
1962	Stanley Cohen discovers epidermal growth factor.
1968	Levi-Montalcini is elected to the National Academy of Sciences.

1969	Levi-Montalcini's research unit becomes part of the Laboratory for Cell Biology; Levi-Montalcini is made director of the whole laboratory.
1969–1972	Abandons research on NGF and studies the nervous system of cockroaches
1971	Ralph Bradshaw and Ruth Hogue Angeletti determine the amino acid sequence of the NGF protein.
early 1970s	The receptor molecule for NGF is identified.
late 1970s	Researchers find a link between NGF and the endocrine system.
1977	Levi-Montalcini's laboratory shows that NGF affects mast cells, part of the immune system; Levi-Montalcini retires from Washington University.
1979	Retires from directorship of the Laboratory for Cell Biology but continues working there as a guest researcher
1983	Researchers identify the gene that carries the code for NGF.
1984	Scientists show that NGF can affect cells in the brain.
1986	Levi-Montalcini and Cohen win the Lasker Award and the Nobel Prize in physiology or medicine.
1987	Awarded the U.S. National Medal of Science
1988	Publishes her autobiography, *In Praise of Imperfection*

late 1980s	Levi-Montalcini and her coworkers find rises in NGF levels in mice undergoing stress.
1990	Proposes that NGF is a key link between the nervous, endocrine, and immune systems
early 1990s	With her twin sister, Levi-Montalcini founds the Rita Levi-Montalcini Onlus Foundation, a charity.
1997	Edits *The Saga of the Nerve Growth Factor,* an anthology of key papers on NGF
1999	Honored in a public celebration of her 90th birthday
2001	Made a life member of the Italian Senate; Howard Federoff's research team finds evidence that NGF stimulates learning in mice.
early 2000s	Founds the European Brain Research Institute
2005	Italian researchers show that in humans, romantic love raises levels of NGF in the blood; Mark Tuszynski reports that putting cells genetically engineered to produce NGF into the brains of Alzheimer's disease patients slows the progress of the disease.

adrenal glands   a pair of glands above the kidneys that secrete a number of different hormones, including those that prepare the body for fight or flight in response to stress

Alzheimer's disease   a common illness, mainly affecting elderly people, in which neurons in parts of the brain are destroyed, producing dementia (mental confusion) and severe memory loss

amino acid   one of 20 types of small molecules that are combined to make proteins

anatomy   the study of the body's structure

angiogenesis   development of new blood vessels

antibodies   substances produced by the immune system that attach to and destroy particular foreign substances, such as bacteria or viruses

apoptosis   programmed cell death

autoimmune diseases   a group of illnesses in which the immune system mistakenly attacks the body's own cells

axon   the long fiber extending from a neuron (nerve cell)

central nervous system   the brain and spinal cord

dendrites   short fibers extending from a neuron (nerve cell)

developmental biology   the scientific field that studies the development of living things both before and after birth

diabetes   an illness caused by the body's failure to produce or to respond to the hormone insulin

differentiate   mature into a specific type of cell, such as a nerve cell or a bone cell

DNA (deoxyribonucleic acid)   the substance of which the genes of most living things are made

embryology   the scientific field that studies development before birth; it is now considered part of developmental biology

endocrine system   the system of glands that produce hormones

enzyme   one of many types of proteins that speed up or make possible chemical reactions within cells, without themselves being involved in the reactions

epidermal growth factor (EGF)   a growth factor, discovered by Stanley Cohen in 1962, that stimulates growth in the outer layer of the skin (epidermis) and related tissues

ganglion   a clump of nerve cells; rows of ganglia (plural of *ganglion*) lie on either side of the spinal cord, among other places

genetic engineering   the process of modifying or moving genes, for instance by transferring them from one type of organism to another

genome   an organism's complete collection of genes

gland   an organ that makes a hormone or hormones

growth factor   one of a group of biochemicals that stimulate growth and other activities in particular types of cells

hippocampus   a part of the forebrain, located in the medial temporal lobe; it plays a role in memory and spatial learning

histology   the study of the microscopic structure of tissues

homeostasis   the body's attempts to keep its internal conditions the same, regardless of changes in its environment

hormone   a substance produced in one part of the body, usually a gland, that affects cells in another part

hypothalamus   a part of the brain involved in responding to stress; when it detects stressful conditions, it orders the pituitary and other glands to secrete hormones that prepare the body for defensive action

immune system   the body's defense system, consisting of a variety of cells (mostly in the blood) and biochemicals

inflammation   redness, swelling, and pain in a part of the body, caused by an immune reaction in that location

insulin   a hormone, made by special cells in the pancreas (a digestive organ), that helps the body manage its storage and use of sugar for energy; its absence (or the loss of ability to respond to it) causes diabetes

in vitro   literally "in glass"; in tissue culture

mast cells   cells of the immune system, particularly involved in allergies; they were the first immune cells shown to respond to NGF

molecular biology   the study of the structure and function of biological molecules and of the biology of the cell at the molecular level

mutation   an alteration in a gene

nerve growth factor (NGF)   a biochemical, discovered by Rita Levi-Montalcini in 1952, that is necessary for the survival and growth of certain kinds of nerves; it also affects a number of other tissues

neurodegenerative disease   a disease that features the breakdown of nerves in the central or peripheral nervous system; examples include Alzheimer's disease and Parkinson's disease

neuron   a nerve cell

neurotransmitter   one of a group of biochemicals that carry signals from one nerve cell to another

nucleic acid   one of two compounds, DNA (deoxyribonucleic acid) and RNA (ribonucleic acid), that carry genetic information in cells

oncogene   a gene that, when active, can cause cancer; oncogenes are mutated forms of normal cell genes, including genes for growth factors and their receptors

Parkinson's disease   a disease of unknown cause in which cells in certain parts of the brain are destroyed, resulting in problems with movement and, sometimes, with thought

pituitary gland   a gland deep inside the brain that secretes hormones, most of which, in turn, stimulate other glands to produce their own hormones; the pituitary also secretes growth hormone

protein   one of a large class of biochemicals that do most of the work in cells; they are long, complexly folded chains of smaller molecules called amino acids

psychoneuroimmunology   a scientific field that studies the relationship between the brain and the immune system and between emotions and physical health

receptor   a molecule, often found on the surface of cells, that fits a particular signaling molecule; when a signaling molecule and its receptor attach or bind to one another, they begin groups of chemical reactions that can have profound effects on the cell

RNA (ribonucleic acid)   one of two nucleic acids that carries genetic information in cells; only certain viruses have genes made of RNA, but various forms of RNA, copied from DNA, can carry out actions ordered by genes, such as making proteins

salivary gland   one of several glands in the mouths of mammals that produce a fluid that helps to begin digestion; in some animals they make other substances as well

sensory neuron   a nerve cell that detects conditions in the environment and sends messages about these conditions to the central nervous system

stress   a perceived threat to an organism from its environment

sympathetic neuron   a nerve cell in the system of nerves that controls automatic actions such as heartbeat and blood flow

synapse   the microscopic gap between the axon ending of one nerve cell and the dendrites of the next cell; neurotransmitters convey signals from one neuron to another across this gap

tissue culture   the process of keeping cells and tissues alive in laboratory containers such as dishes or tubes

vascular endothelial growth factor (VEGF)   a growth factor that stimulates the growth of new blood vessels

FURTHER RESOURCES

Books

Dash, Joan. *The Triumph of Discovery: Women Scientists Who Won the Nobel Prize.* New York: Julian Messner, 1991.

> *For young adults. Includes a chapter on Levi-Montalcini.*

Hargittai, István. *Candid Science II: Conversations with Famous Biomedical Scientists.* London: Imperial College Press, 2002.

> *Contains a interview with Levi-Montalcini done in 2000, including her comments about seeing science from the point of view of an artist.*

Hitchcock, Susan Tyler. *Rita Levi-Montalcini: Nobel Prize Winner.* New York: Chelsea House, 2004.

> *Biography of Levi-Montalcini for young adults.*

Levi-Montalcini, Rita, tr. Luigi Attardi. *In Praise of Imperfection: My Life and Work.* New York: Basic Books, 1988.

> *Levi-Montalcini's autobiography, including accounts of her wartime work in her home laboratory in Italy and her discovery of nerve growth factor during research at Washington University.*

———. "NGF: An Uncharted Route." In Frederic G. Worden et al., eds. *The Neurosciences: Paths of Discovery.* Cambridge, Mass.: MIT Press, 1975.

> *Autobiographical chapter in book on neuroscience written primarily for scientists.*

———. "Reflections on a Scientific Adventure." In Derek Richter, ed. *Women Scientists: The Road to Liberation.* London: Macmillan, 1982.

> *Autobiographical chapter in book on the experiences of women scientists.*

———. ed. *The Saga of the Nerve Growth Factor: Preliminary Studies, Discovery, Further Development.* River Edge, N.J.: World Scientific, 1997.

*Collection of key scientific papers on nerve growth factor pub-
lished between 1942 and 1995 by Levi-Montalcini and others,
edited and with comments by Levi-Montalcini.*

"Levi-Montalcini, Rita." In *Current Biography Yearbook 1989.* New
York: H. W. Wilson, 1989.

*Detailed biographical profile of Levi-Montalcini, based on
interviews and other printed sources published before 1989.*

McGrayne, Sharon Bertsch. *Nobel Prize Women in Science: Their Lives,
Struggles, and Momentous Discoveries, 2nd ed.* Washington, D.C.:
Joseph Henry Press and National Academy of Sciences, 2001.

*For young adults. Contains a long chapter on Levi-Montalcini,
including numerous quotations from her and from people who
knew her.*

Internet Resources

Baker, Mitzi. "Finding May Unlock Secret to Nerve Growth Factor."
Stanford Report, May 26, 2004. Available online. URL: http://news-
service.stanford.edu/news/medical/2004/may26/nerve.html. Accessed
March 5, 2008.

*Short report on two Stanford researchers, Xiao-lin He and Chris
Garcia, who worked out the three-dimensional structure that the
nerve growth factor takes on when it binds with its receptors.*

Garfield, Eugene. "Stanley Cohen's and Rita Levi-Montalcini's Discoveries
of Growth Factors Lead to 1986 Nobel in Medicine." Essays of an
Information Scientist, Current Comments, April 27, 1987. Available
online. URL: www.garfield.library.upenn.edu/essays/v10p106y1987.pdf.
Accessed March 5, 2008.

Essay by the editor of Scientist *magazine describes Levi-
Montalcini's and Cohen's research and its impact in terms of
citations of their papers made by other scientists.*

Hall, Kerstin. "The Nobel Prize in Physiology or Medicine 1986:
Presentation Speech." Nobelprize.org, 1986. Available online. URL:
http://nobelprize.org/nobel_prizes/medicine/laureates/1986/presenta
tion-speech.html. Accessed March 5, 2008.

*Speech given before presentation of the 1986 Nobel Prize in physi-
ology or medicine to Rita Levi-Montalcini and Stanley Cohen
discusses the importance of their discovery of growth factors.*

King, Michael W., and Sergio Marchesini. "Growth Factors and Cytokines." Facoltà di Medicina e Chirurgia, Universitá degli studi di Brescia (Italy), last updated January 9, 2008. Available online. URL: http://www.med.unibs.it/~marchesi/growfact.html. Accessed March 5, 2008.

Paper for scientists, in English, describes the principal growth factors and their effects on cells and the body.

Levi-Montalcini, Rita. "Autobiography." Nobelprize.org, 1986. Available online. URL: http://nobelprize.org/nobel_prizes/medicine/laureates/1986/levi-montalcini-autobio.html. Accessed March 5, 2008.

Brief autobiographical sketch written by Levi-Montalcini at the time she received the Nobel Prize in physiology or medicine in 1986.

———. "The Nerve Growth Factor: 35 Years Later." Nobelprize.org, 1986. Available online. URL: http://nobelprize.org/nobel_prizes/medicine/laureates/1986/levi-montalcini-lecture.html. Accessed March 5, 2008.

Lecture that Levi-Montalcini gave in Sweden after receiving the 1986 Nobel Prize in physiology or medicine describes her work and its implications in technical detail.

Tuszynski, Mark. "Gene Therapy for Alzheimer's Disease—Clinical Trial Updates." Tuszynski laboratory, University of California at San Diego, updated January 25, 2008. Available online. URL: http://tuszynskilab.ucsd.edu/gt.php. Accessed March 5, 2008.

Describes research in which cells from patients' own skin, genetically engineered to produce nerve growth factor, were inserted into the brains of small numbers of people with Alzheimer's disease. The treatment appeared to slow the progress of the disease.

Periodicals

Aloe, Luigi, and Rita Levi-Montalcini. "Mast Cells Increase in Tissues of Neonatal Rats Injected with the Nerve Growth Factor." *Brain Research,* vol. 133 (1977), pp. 358–366.

This article reports the first link between nerve growth factor and the immune system by showing that NGF causes the numbers of a type of immune system cell, the mast cell, to increase.

Brooks, Andrew I., et al. "Enhanced Learning in Mice Parallels Vector-Mediated Nerve Growth Factor Expression in Hippocampus." *Human Gene Therapy,* vol. 17 (2000), pp. 2,341–2,352.

Brooks and his coworkers found that mice given a combination of gene therapy to increase the amount of NGF in their brains and stimulation by constant new learning experiences learned new mazes more quickly than mice given either treatment alone. Their work suggests that NGF plays a role in helping people and animals learn.

Brune, Brett. "Nobel Laureate Comes to Aid of Women in Ethiopia." *St. Louis Post-Dispatch,* November 21, 2004, p. A15.

Describes the Rita Levi-Montalcini Onlus Foundation, which helps to educate young women in Ethiopia.

Bueker, Elmer D. "Implantation of Tumors in the Hind Limb Field of the Embryonic Chick and the Developmental Response of the Lumbosacral Nervous System." *Anatomical Records,* vol. 102 (1948), pp. 369–389.

This article, which reported that one type of mouse tumor produced unusual nerve growth in chick embryos, inspired Levi-Montalcini to investigate this growth further and led to her discovery of nerve growth factor.

Cohen, Stanley, Rita Levi-Montalcini, and Viktor Hamburger. "A Nerve Growth-Stimulating Factor Isolated from Sarcomas 37 and 180." *Proceedings of the National Academy of Sciences (USA),* vol. 40 (1954), pp. 1,014–1,018.

Article in which nerve growth factor was given its name and characterized chemically for the first time. Cohen concluded that the factor appeared to be a combination of nucleic acid and protein.

Colangelo, Anna M., et al. "Recombinant Human Nerve Growth Factor with a Marked Activity in Vitro and in Vivo." *Proceedings of the National Academy of Sciences (USA),* vol. 102 (2005), pp. 8,658–8,663.

This article is the most recent scientific paper bearing Rita Levi-Montalcini's name (as a coauthor).

Emanuele, Enzo, et al. "Raised Plasma Nerve Growth Factor Levels Associated with Early-Stage Romantic Love." *Psychoneuroendocrinology* (April 2006), pp. 31–33.

Scientific article reports that levels of nerve growth factor were significantly higher than normal in the blood of 58 volunteers between the ages of 18 and 31 who defined themselves as being newly in love, but the levels went back to normal after a year, even if the relationships continued.

Hamburger, Viktor. "The Effects of Wing Bud Extirpation on the Development of the Central Nervous System in Chick Embryos." *Journal of Experimental Zoology*, vol. 68 (1934), pp. 449–494.

> *The article that inspired Rita Levi-Montalcini's research in her home laboratory from 1940 to 1942*

Holloway, Marguerite. "Finding the Good in the Bad." *Scientific American* (January 1993), pp. 32, 36.

> *Biographical profile of Levi-Montalcini and summary of her work, written several years after she won the Nobel Prize.*

Kahn, Carol. "Tapping the Healers Within." *Omni* (March 1988), pp. 37–38, 96–102.

> *Describes the discovery of growth factors and their present (in the late 1980s) and possible future uses in medicine.*

Kimata, Hajime. "Laughter Counteracts Enhancement of Plasma Neurotrophin Levels and Allergic Skin Wheal Responses by Mobile Phone-Mediated Stress." *Behavioral Medicine* (Winter 2004), pp. 149–152.

> *Explains that stress induced by writing text messages on a cell phone raised blood levels of NGF and related substances and increased the intensity of allergic reactions in people with atopic dermatitis, an allergy-related skin ailment. Laughter induced by watching a humorous video lowered the raised levels, but watching a video of weather information did not.*

Levi-Montalcini, Rita. "From Turin to Stockholm via St. Louis and Rio de Janeiro." *Science* (February 4, 2000), p. 89.

> *Levi-Montalcini recalls the highlights of her life and scientific career.*

———. "The Origin and Development of the Visceral System in the Spinal Cord of the Chick Embryo." *Journal of Morphology*, vol. 86 (1950), pp. 253–284.

> *In this article, Levi-Montalcini describes her 1947 discovery that cell death and migration as well as growth are normal parts of the development of the embryonic chick's nervous system.*

———, Luigi Aloe, and Enrico Alleva. "A Role for Nerve Growth Factor in Nervous, Endocrine and Immune Systems." *Progress in Neuroendocrinimmunology*, vol. 3 (1990), pp. 1–10.

> *This article links three of the body's most important systems—the nervous, endocrine (hormonal), and immune systems—through*

the actions of nerve growth factor. Levi-Montalcini speculates that NGF helps the body prepare to defend and maintain itself in the face of threats from the environment.

————, and Pietro U. Angeletti. "Immunosympathectomy." *Pharmacological Reviews,* vol. 18 (1966), pp. 619–629.

Levi-Montalcini and Angeletti, who became Levi-Montalcini's chief coworker after the departure of Stanley Cohen, report that giving newborn mice an antiserum to nerve growth factor essentially destroys their sympathetic nervous system.

————, and Barbara Booker. "Excessive Growth of the Sympathetic Ganglia Evoked by a Protein Isolated from Mouse Salivary Glands." *Proceedings of the National Academy of Sciences (USA),* vol. 46 (1960), pp. 373–384.

Levi-Montalcini, Stanley Cohen, and graduate student Booker report on a new source for nerve growth factor: the salivary glands of male mice.

————, and Stanley Cohen. "In Vitro and In Vivo Effects of a Nerve Growth-Stimulating Agent Isolated from Snake Venom." *Proceedings of the National Academy of Sciences (USA),* vol. 42 (1956), pp. 695–699.

In this article, Levi-Montalcini and Cohen report their discovery that snake venom contains nerve growth factor and describe the factor's effects on whole animals and on cells in culture.

————, and Giuseppe Levi. "Les conséquences de la destruction d'un territoire d'innervation périphérique sur le dévelopment des centres nerveux correspondants dans l'embryon de poulet." *Archives de Biologie,* vol. 53 (1942), pp. 537–535.

The original article in which Levi-Montalcini described the work she did in her "Robinson Crusoe" home laboratory. In French.

————, Hertha Meyer, and Viktor Hamburger. "In Vitro Experiments on the Effects of Mouse Sarcomas 180 and 37 on the Spinal and Sympathetic Ganglia of the Chick Embryo." *Cancer Research,* vol. 14 (1953), pp. 49–57.

Describes Levi-Montalcini's tissue culture research in Rio de Janeiro, in which she showed that a substance produced by these mouse tumors made nerve cells grow vigorously in tissue culture, just as it did in whole chick embryos.

Liversidge, Anthony. "Interview: Rita Levi-Montalcini." *Omni* (March 1988), pp. 70–74, 102–105.

Extensive interview with Levi-Montalcini describes her scientific work, including research that took place after she returned to Italy in the 1960s.

Marx, Jean L. "The 1986 Nobel Prize for Physiology or Medicine." *Science* (October 31, 1986), pp. 543–544.

Briefly describes Rita Levi-Montalcini and Stanley Cohen's discovery of the first growth factors, which led to their receiving the prestigious prize.

McGuire, John M. "Queen of Italy in a Lab Coat: Nobel Prize-winning Scientist Revisits her Research Home." *St. Louis Post-Dispatch,* January 16, 2003.

Article written on the occasion of a visit to St. Louis by Levi-Montalcini portrays her personality through the words of people who knew her when she worked at Washington University.

Randall, Frederika. "The Heart and Mind of a Genius." *Vogue* (March 1987), pp. 480, 536.

Brief profile of Levi-Montalcini.

Rohrlich, Ruby. "Jewish Lives: Rita Levi-Montalcini." *Judaism: A Quarterly Journal of Jewish Life and Thought* (Winter 2000), pp. 36ff.

Extensive biographical portrait of Levi-Montalcini, based largely on her autobiography.

Seiler, M., and M. Schwab. "Specific Retrograde Transport of Nerve Growth Factor (NGF) from Neocortex to Nucleus Basalis in the Rat." *Research,* vol. 300 (1984), pp. 33–39.

This article was the first report showing that nerve growth factor affects the brain.

Williams, Nigel. "Newspaper Backs Down over Allegations of Impropriety." *Science* (September 22, 1995), pp. 1,663–1,664.

Describes accusations by a Swedish newspaper that Levi-Montalcini won the 1986 Nobel Prize in physiology or medicine because of a "gigantic campaign" by Fidia, an Italian pharmaceutical company, to influence members of the Nobel committee. The newspaper retracted some of its statements after intense criticism.

INDEX